You Might Be A Crazy Cat Lady If...

By Janet Vormittag

You Might Be A Crazy Cat Lady If...

Photographs by Janet Vormittag.

Cover design by Sierra Cole.
www.sierracole.com

Ernie (Ernie, Ernesto and Emma, page 59) is the kitty on the cover.

Some names have been changed for privacy protection.

ISBN: 978-0-9986987-0-0

JLV Enterprises LLC
Cats and Dogs

Janet Vormittag
P.O. Box 996
Jenison, MI 49429-0996

janetvormittag.com

Printed in Michigan, USA.

Dedicated to Lucy, the cat who started it all,
and to all the people who love cats.

A special thanks to Nina Bloomfield, Lee Bradley, Leonard Campbell, Sierra Cole, Melissa Eefsting, Pat Pritchard, Gayle Thompson and my fellow writers in Sweet Potato Fries and Monday Night Writers.

Also by Janet Vormittag

Dog 281

More Than a Number

Contents

Introduction

When asked as a child, "What do you want to be when you grow up?" I remember shrugging my shoulders and saying, "I don't know."

I didn't know. I hadn't given it any thought. I should have. I should have given it a lot of thought. I admit to never having a plan for my life, no goals. Instead, I wandered aimlessly, squandering time and taking the path of least resistance. Now here I am, some 50 years later. Worried. Worried about what I might have become—a crazy cat lady. But I don't really think I'm crazy—I've always hated that label. I prefer *compassionate* cat lady.

But I know I'm not alone. For the last ten years I have published a monthly magazine, *Cats and Dogs, a Magazine Devoted to Companion Animals*. I have met countless crazy cat ladies (and crazy dog ladies), but I always say they're crazy in a good way.

Are you one of them? See if you say yes to any of the following statements.

You might be a crazy cat lady if ...

___ The last thing you do before you leave the house is check yourself for cat hair. And when you do leave, you say goodbye and tell your four-legged friends when you'll be back.

___ You can't say no when someone asks you to foster kittens or cats.

___ You adopt the kittens or cats you're supposed to be fostering.

___ Kittens and cats appear out of nowhere. In bushes at restaurants, on hiking trails or on your porch, in your barn and yard.

___ For birthdays and Christmases, 99 percent of the gifts you receive have something to do with cats: cat T-shirts, cat books, cat knick-knacks, cat stationery, catnip, cat magazines, cat buttons, cat lawn ornaments, cat jewelry, cat magnets, cat coffee cups ... the possibilities are endless.

___ You spend a year taming a feral cat.

___ Instead of photographs of smiling children in your wallet, on your phone, on your refrigerator or hanging on your walls, you have photographs of your cats.

___ You were horrified the first time you heard the word ringworm, but now it doesn't faze you.

___ You go to an animal shelter to pick up four kittens and leave with 16 kittens.

___ You spend more money on cat food than you do people food.

___ Your home has empty cardboard boxes tucked in out-of-the-way places for your cats to play in.

___ The largest piece of furniture in your living room is a Cat Mountain designed with perches and cubby holes.

___ You quit feeding birds because you realize bird feeders

are actually cat feeders.

___ You get calls from friends and family when a stray cat shows up in their yard. You get the same call from distant relatives, neighbors you've never met, friends of friends, and unknown co-workers.

___ You have two or more black cats and love Halloween because stores are full of black cat decorations.

___ You share your home with semi-feral cats who are seldom seen.

___ You go to a garage sale and the only thing you come home with is a kitten.

___ You cover your furniture with blankets or afghans to cover where cats have shredded the upholstery.

___ Your home décor is American Domestic Feline.

___ Mice who dare enter your home have a short life span.

___ When you are asked how many cats you have, you're tempted to lie, but instead you laugh and divert the question.

___ The repairman who's working on your gas fireplace asks if you're missing a cat as he vacuums cat hair out of the blower, which is the only reason the fireplace quit working.

___ You turn on the space heater in the bathroom and it emits a smoldering, skunk-like odor, which you immediately recognize as burnt cat pee.

___ Your computer quits working. You drop it off for repairs and the next day they call and ask, "Do you have a cat?"

___ You have your own pet cemetery with flowers and concrete cat statues marking the graves.

Lucy, the partially paralyzed cat, who started my obsession with felines.

LUCY

You might be a crazy cat lady if ... instead of photographs of smiling children in your wallet, on your phone, on your refrigerator or hanging on your walls, you have photographs of cats.

My obsession began with Lucy, a black and white tuxedo kitty. I had other cats, but they were just cats. When I should have been thinking babies and perpetuating my genetic traits, I was mothering a physically challenged cat. My days began with Lucy and ended with her. I worried about her. I dreaded vacations because it meant being separated from her. When I looked into her eyes I saw an old soul—I felt she knew things I couldn't comprehend.

Lucy came into my life on a September day when my husband, Mark, and I traveled to Saugatuck for a romantic Lake Michigan sunset. The first thing we heard when we stepped out of the van was a mournful cry.

"It's a bird," I said.

"No, it's a cat," Mark claimed as the soulful wail echoed between the sand dune and the Kalamazoo River. We looked around but couldn't find who was crying.

It was off-season and Mount Baldhead, with its 282 wooden steps to the top of a bluff overlooking the Great Lake, was deserted. We climbed about a dozen stairs when Mark turned around and looked back at the parking lot.

"I told you it was a cat," he said pointing to a bush. He was right. We turned around and were soon peering under the shrub at a black and white kitten.

"Here kitty, kitty," I called, holding out my hand in friendship.

The kitten, a tiny thing, dragged herself to us. She was bloated like a half-inflated balloon. She wasn't moving her back legs. Sand fleas were hopping all over her, yet she purred, a deep rumbling purr.

Mark gently turned her over and she still purred. There were no cuts, no open wounds, no sign of injury, but there was definitely something wrong.

"Now what do we do?" I asked. "We just can't leave her here."

It was after Labor Day and the tourist town was winding down its summer season. I knocked on the doors of a few nearby cottages, but only one showed signs of life. A woman opened the door.

"Hi, my husband and I found a black and white kitten at the park next door. Is it yours? Do you know who it belongs to?"

"No. Is that what we've heard crying all day?"

"Probably."

"Sorry, I don't know anything about a cat. We're just

renting, and we're leaving tomorrow."

I thanked her and went back to the park. A young couple came stomping down the stairs; I asked if they knew anything about the kitten. The woman said they had seen it earlier, but her boyfriend hated cats. He didn't even stop walking as she answered my question. She hurriedly joined him and they climbed into a pickup truck.

"No luck," I said to Mark.

"What do you want to do?"

"Take her home, I guess. We can't leave her here."

I had a cardboard box and clean rags in the van; together they made a makeshift cat carrier. Once home, I fixed the kitten an area for the night with a blanket, food, water and a litter box all placed inside a huge cardboard box. Every time I checked the cat-in-the-box she was sprawled in the litter.

Fortunately, I had the next day off work. Our vet, Dr. Meyers, was able to see me and the kitten between appointments. He gently examined the misshapen babe, and then took a needle and pricked her tail. She howled.

"That's good. Her back isn't broken."

He picked her up and said he'd return in a few minutes. I waited.

Finally he came back with a diagnosis. The bloat was due to a bladder packed with urine. The young cat was partially paralyzed, resulting in an inability to urinate, defecate or walk.

"I squeezed her bladder and can't believe how much urine I got out of her," he said. "She wouldn't have lived much longer without being relieved."

"What does that mean?"

Doc didn't know if she would recover the use of her bowels, bladder or back legs. He said he could put her down or I could take her home and see what happened.

The options weren't really options at all. I took her home, but only after a lesson in cat anatomy with an emphasis on the bladder.

"When it's full it'll feel like a 40-watt light bulb," Dr. Meyers explained. "When you find it, gently squeeze. Make sure you're gentle."

When Mark came home from work that night, I repeated Dr. Meyers' instructions. He didn't say anything, but his silence gave me the impression he thought I chose the wrong option. When I couldn't find the elusive light bulb, he was willing to try. He couldn't find it either, and the next day found Mark getting a first-hand lesson from Dr. Meyers.

That night while I held the kitten's front half, Mark pointed the back end into the kitchen sink, but he couldn't locate the bladder.

"I'll try it again," I said. We switched positions. I caressed her head with one hand while feeling and squeezing her belly with the other hand. All of sudden Lucy stiffened. Something was happening.

"Oh no, she's pooping in the sink," I screamed.

"Don't worry, I'll clean it up."

After she emptied her bowels, I easily found the bladder. From then on I was an expert at emptying it.

Lucy was a sweet spirit, never complaining. I put a litter box in the spare bedroom. Three times a day I emptied her bladder. Fortunately she gained control of her bowels, but getting into the litter box was a problem. I solved it by spreading newspapers on the floor around the box. Every day she left me a pile of poop.

Lucy finally was able to pee on her own, but never in the litter box, always on the newspapers. She never was able to walk. Instead she dragged herself around using her front legs. She flew on the oak floors, keeping them polished to a high sheen. She'd sink her front claws into the couch like a mountaineer sinking a pickax into ice and pull herself up like a climber scaling a mountain.

Lucy loved anything and everything soft: an afghan, a sweater or a fuzzy blanket. She'd either sink her claws into it and pull it to the floor or scale the furniture to get to it. Either way, she'd cuddle into it, knead it with her front claws and purr. She had a purr like the rumble of a distant train.

Lucy also dragged herself out the dog door. Once in the outside pen, she'd squeeze between the fence and house and explore the yard. I often found her in an unkempt part of the backyard that I called 'the jungle.' It was shaded by a huge weeping willow, and the ground was a maze of critter trails among thigh-high weeds, wild flowers and willow branches.

Lucy would anchor herself beside a rodent trail and wait. She had the patience of a hunter.

Always the worrier, I never left Lucy outside alone. I'd weed the flowerbeds, pick up sticks or sometimes just pull up a lounge chair and read. Once when I was working in front of the house, I heard a loud commotion coming from the backyard. I ran to find Lucy—she was easy to spot. Two birds were repeatedly dive bombing her.

"Get out of here. Go!" I screamed as I waved my arms.

As I got closer, I realized why the birds were attacking her. There she sat with a bird in her mouth and a smug look on her face. The only way she could have caught a bird was if it had fallen out of a nest and landed near her, or if the unlucky fledgling was attempting its first flight.

I grabbed her by the neck. "Let it go," I said. I repeated the command over and over until she dropped it.

The young bird was breathing, and I didn't see any wounds. I picked up Lucy and carried her into the house letting the parent birds rescue their baby.

All my motherly instincts focused on Lucy. She was my first chore each morning and the last thing I checked before going to bed. Mark and I slept upstairs, and Lucy couldn't do steps. Every morning she waited for me at the bottom of the stairs.

Lucy's injury made her prone to bladder infections. She'd go to her newspapers and strain to pee, but nothing would come out. A few minutes later she'd repeat the attempt, and I'd know it was time to visit Dr. Meyers again. She'd come home with liquid antibiotics and a lack of appetite.

"You have to eat," I'd tell her. She'd sniff the turkey bits in gravy and look away. "Eat," I'd repeat in a stern voice. If she absolutely refused, I'd try a new flavor or open a can of tuna fish. She'd gingerly pick at whatever delicacy I dished up.

During this time, I was enrolled in a photography class at Grand Valley State University. We worked in black and white and learned to develop and print our own photos. Like anyone with a child, Lucy was the star of the majority of my photos. One of my prized possessions is a double-exposure print of Lucy in the sky. No diamonds, just my Lucy.

My double exposure print of Lucy, which was an assignment in a photography class.

My refrigerator is a gallery for part of my
collection of cat magnets.

Cat Collecting

You might be a crazy cat lady if ... for birthdays and Christmases, 99 percent of the gifts you receive have something to do with cats: cat T-shirts, cat books, cat knick-knacks, cat stationery, catnip, cat magazines, cat buttons, cat lawn ornaments, cat jewelry, cat magnets, cat towels, cat coffee cups—the possibilities are endless.

"Oh, they're magnets! How cool," I said as I opened the Christmas gift my sister-in-law had mailed from New Orleans. I promptly stuck the set of cats—three black and one white—on the refrigerator. The little family, about an inch tall and carved of wood, looked lonely on the big Frigidaire. Soon afterwards, I noticed a display of magnets at a gift store and found myself searching for a cat. Thus, the birth of a new hobby—collecting cat magnets.

The New Orleans kitties are no longer lonely. They have buddies made of enamel, ceramic, clay, glass, plastic, cardboard and metal. Some are quite famous, like the reproductions of paintings: *The Cat and Mouse in Partnership* by British artist Arthur Rackham, *Cats* by French artist Theophile Alexandre Steinlen and *The Large Cat* by Dutch artist Cornelis Visscher.

My travels over the years have been documented by cat magnets. In San Francisco, I was elated to find a magnet of a tabby cat perched on the Golden Gate Bridge and titled 'San Franciscat.' Another cat, #704622, behind bars and sporting striped black and white prison attire, was labeled 'Al Catraz.' From the Hemingway Home and Museum in Key West, I bought a magnet with a photograph of two polydactyl kittens climbing on an old manual typewriter. Author Ernest Hemingway was known for his love of cats, and descendants of his extra-toe fur-friends still roam the grounds of his former home at the tip of Florida.

Some of my favorite magnets are humorous, such as the sketch of a dog chained to a doghouse and saying to a cat, "They don't keep you leashed because they want you to run away." Or two cats in a classroom sitting at desks with '2 + 2 = __' written on the chalkboard. The caption reads 'Against Animal Testing.'

Sayings are also popular, such as the old Native American Proverb: *After dark all cats are leopards.* Or, Cat Rule #3: *There are no stray cats, cats always know where they are going.* Or, *No outfit is complete without cat hair.*

Not only is my refrigerator plastered with cat magnets, so is the four-drawer metal filing cabinet in my office. Personally, I think the bland metal repositories are enhanced by the collection. They mesmerize houseguests.

Unfortunately, magnets were only the beginning. The next Christmas Mark gave me a 12-inch-tall gray and black striped ceramic cat. When his sister came to visit from

Chicago, she arrived with a birthday gift: a three-foot-tall, fiberglass fat cat seat-belted in the passenger seat of her car. I loved it. The weatherproof statue found a new home on the porch outside the sliding glass door. In the winter, he's quite handsome decked out in snow, and in the summer he's surrounded with flowers.

Mark preferred the collection be contained in my office, but you know how cats are. They're independent, don't follow directions and tend to multiply. Feed one stray and the next thing you know he's inviting his buddies over for a free meal, and his girlfriends are having kittens. Soon there are grand-kittens and the house is overrun.

I truly believe friends and family have fun shopping for cats for me, but I can't blame it all on them. For years, my every shopping expedition was cat-obsessed—my house is proof.

The walls of the staircase going to the room above the garage, which is my office, are covered with cat art. At the top of the steps are curio shelves filled with a menagerie of cat figurines—gifts, garage-sale treasures, flea-market finds and gift store trinkets.

A foyer curio cabinet is devoted to Mexican felines, ceramic kitties hand painted with local scenery from our sun-drenched neighbor to the south. For years, Mark and I were snowbirds in the Mayan Riviera—sun, beaches, hammocks, sightseeing, an all-you-can-eat resort and *shopping*.

While the cat collecting obsession has cooled, it hasn't been extinguished. Just last month I was invited to see the play *Cats* at Circle Theater. I've seen the production twice before. This time they were selling silver, diamond-studded, cat ear headbands and a cool purple *Cats* poster. I bought one of each.

Part of my collection of cats bought during Mexican vacations.

The fat-cat birthday gift that has permanent residence on my deck.

The live-trap used for catching mice.

Trophy Tails

You might be a crazy cat lady if ... mice who dare enter your home have a short life span.

Cool weather was settling in and mice sought shelter in our turn-of-the-century farmhouse with its cracks and gaps that rodents could squeeze and wiggle through in search of warmth. Unfortunately for them, Lucy was a born hunter. What she lost in mobility with paralyzed back legs, she made up for with patience. She could out-wait any mouse.

As a vegetarian with compassion for all life, I bought a Havahart Mouse Trap—a gray, plastic, rectangular box that teeter-tottered. When tilted with the weight of a rodent, its trapdoor would snap shut, capturing any critter who ventured inside for the bait.

One day while studying at the kitchen table, I heard an unfamiliar sound. Looking up, I spotted a mouse. A chunk of dry dog food was gripped in his teeth as he scurried away from the dog's food bowl. The little guy squeezed through a crack and disappeared under a kitchen cabinet. A few seconds later he reappeared and scored another snack. While he was storing his bounty the second time, I picked up the food bowl and replaced it with a dog-food baited Havahart trap. Mr. Mouse returned, sniffed around the trap, making circles around it in search of his gold mine of kibble. I could feel his confusion. *Where did it go? I swear this is where it was.* Mr. Mouse finally detected the lone nugget tucked in the gray box. I held my breath. He hesitated, but greed won. He went in. The trap tilted and he was mine. I carried the trapped rodent across the road and let him loose in the woods.

"Be free," I said, "and don't come back."

One Sunday evening while watching TV, I noticed Lucy wasn't in her usual spot—sitting next to me on the couch, on her blanket, kneading and purring. Instead, she sat on the floor, staring at the piano. I called her name. She ignored me.

"Is there a mouse under the piano?" I asked. I started paying more attention to Lucy than I did to *60 Minutes*.

When the mouse finally darted out, Lucy moved like a leopard, swift and merciless. I screamed, jumped up, grabbed her (and her mouse), and carried her out the front door.

"Let it go," I said. She refused. I shook her, screaming, "Let it go!" Finally she dropped it. The mouse scurried off, and I brought Lucy back inside. She sniffed around the piano, and then came to the couch and pulled herself up. She dragged herself to her blanket, started kneading its softness and began to purr.

During that autumn Lucy and I had a contest of who could catch the most mice. I'd catch and release. Lucy would catch and eat. Her proof of capture was a leftover tail. "What's the problem?" I asked. "Too chewy?"

Her trophy tail was usually presented to me at the bottom of the stairs.

Lucy was a proud hunter, standing guard over the remains until the cleanup crew—me—arrived. I was tempted to tack each tail, at Lucy level, on the landing wall. One thing about old farmhouses, additional holes in the walls only add character. But the thought of the smell and sight of trophy tails stopped me.

That autumn I caught 17 mice. Lucy's count was close to the same. Then the invasion was over, my trap remained empty, and Lucy resorted to store-bought food.

I often wondered: did we really have 30-plus mice invade our home? Or did the mice I set free sneak back into the house only to become Lucy's dinner? Maybe I should have carried them farther away. After it was over, I regretted that I hadn't dipped the tails of my catch in pink paint before setting them free. Then I would have known if having a heart made a difference.

Boomer strolling down the driveway. He climbed ladders and enjoyed viewing the world from the roof of the house.

Boomer and the Great Spraying War

You might be a crazy cat lady if ... you go to a garage sale and the only thing you come home with is a kitten.

The orange and white kitten trotted across the paved street to my sister's garage sale at an inner-city rental house she and her husband were renovating. What was a sweet, little tabby doing out by himself, crossing a city street and walking up to strangers?

The confident imp stole my heart, but I worried about his home life and his future. Who would let such a little guy out on his own? I asked around, but none of the neighbors claimed him. I guessed he was from a litter born under a porch and socialized by neighborhood kids. At the end of the garage sale, the kitten was still hanging out with us, soaking up attention and making friends. I couldn't leave him to fend for himself on the city streets. As I was leaving, I cat-napped him. He would be a country cat.

I don't remember Mark's reaction to my bringing home a kitten, but I do recall how the little guy got his name. Mark was lying on the floor on his stomach watching TV, his arms folded in front of his face. After a long day of hanging out at the sale and finding himself in an unfamiliar environment, the little guy found the perfect place to snuggle: in the crook of Mark's arms. He settled in, and it was the perfect bonding experience. That is until baby let a big boomer. I heard it and soon smelled it. But poor Mark. He *felt* it—a warm soft swoosh of air on his cheek. No doubt baby wasn't used to canned food, which created an upset tummy that produced a wee bit of gas with a horrendous odor. The farts eventually faded, but the name Boomer stuck.

The first time I took Boomer to the vet to get neutered, they sent him home, saying he was too young for the operation. He had to wait a couple weeks. The reason I relay this information is he was "fixed" as soon as possible. Despite his operation, he still took up the bad habit of spraying. I can thank Smokey for teaching him all he knew about being male.

Smokey was an older gray cat. His original home had been a duplex at the end of our dead-end street where he had been the mascot of a house full of college students. His home came to an end when the last student graduated. The graduate claimed he couldn't take Smokey with him and couldn't find another home for the faithful companion. He told his landlord, who happened to be Mark's cousin, that he was going to drop Smokey off at the humane society. She knew the humane society was not a safe place for an older cat—he probably would be euthanized due to his age. So Linda took Smokey and brought him to us.

Smokey was confused for a long time. He'd walk the half-mile to his old home just about every day. Linda, who was cleaning and painting at the duplex, would let him in so he could see his home no longer existed. At the end of her workday, she'd drive him back to our house. The scenario repeated itself until Smokey realized his people and home were gone.

When Boomer came along, Smokey felt threatened by another male and started marking his territory. Boomer thought it looked like great fun and thus began the great spraying war. How high can you get it? The last straw, or shall I say the last spray, was when Smokey sprayed my pants— and I was wearing them; he wanted me as his own. It wasn't to be. The boys were evicted and became barn cats.

Smokey, the sweet old man the neighbors couldn't take with them when they moved.

Maggie was left behind when her people moved. I found homes for her babies and kept her.

Pumpkin and Pearl

You might be a crazy cat lady if ... you share your home with semi-feral cats who are seldom seen.

The summer of 1994 I was on a high from successfully finding homes for four kittens I had inherited when a neighbor moved and neglected to pack his pregnant cat. The left-behind mom-to-be had her babies in a woodpile, but the new owners of the home didn't appreciate the house-warming gift of a cat family.

So guess who got them?

The babies were young enough to be socialized, and by placing a "Homes Needed" poster on my veterinarian's bulletin board, I found families for them. Mom cat became Maggie. She wasn't as easy to place, and I ended up keeping her. Maggie loved food. I attributed her overeating to nursing babies on a starvation diet. My vet called her a nine-pound cat in a seven-pound body.

Finding homes for Maggie's brood had been easy, so I didn't hesitate to say yes to the opportunity to take two kittens who mysteriously appeared in my sister's yard. They were the cutest things I'd ever seen: brown tigers with splotches of the whitest white. There was just one problem: they were wild. They had been living outside with no supervision—climbing trees, chasing bugs and only coming near people to beg for food.

"I'll tame them and find them homes," I said with confidence.

Catching the semi-feral kittens proved to be a challenge. I asked my niece, Jennifer, not to feed the kitties the day I planned to come by and pick them up. My strategy was simple: hunger would entice the little rascals into a cat carrier. It worked except for one thing—they were fast. They went into the carrier, but when I went to close the door, one escaped. The captured kitten went berserk inside its prison, while its littermate ran for cover in the woods. It took patience, tasty treats and sweet-talk to lure the escapee to within grabbing distance.

I took only one carrier, thinking the loving siblings would find comfort with one another during the ride to their new home. I didn't dare open the carrier a second time, so Jennifer had to hold the fugitive tightly in her arms and accompany me home. By the end of the ordeal, we both had battle scratches.

We transferred the terrified kittens into a large wire-mesh cage in the back room of my home. The youngsters probably had never been inside a house, let alone confined to a cage, no matter what its size. They ran in circles, desperately searching for an escape. There wasn't one. But there was a place to hide. I had placed a cardboard box upside down in the cage and cut a cat-size hole in one side of the box. They huddled together in the makeshift cave for days.

They didn't appreciate the trip to the vet to get a checkup or the neuter and spay—I learned I had a brother-sister combo. I gave them the temporary names of Pearl and Pumpkin, thinking their new owners would give them better names.

When I finally let them loose in the house, they disappeared. I realized giving them their freedom had been a mistake, but it was too late. There are a million and one places in an old farmhouse for scared kittens to hide. They even discovered a hole, which I hadn't known existed, in the back of a closet and squeezed through it into the attic. My dream of being a cat whisperer and re-homing the bonded duo faded like a New Year's Resolution.

A few years later, we built a new house behind the decrepit farmhouse. After we moved, the house we had called home for 22 years was torn down. I was able to catch Pumpkin and Pearl and release them in my office, a 400-square-foot room above the garage. The move traumatized them, but they soon found new hiding places among unpacked boxes, under a couch and behind my desk. But I made progress. Pearl finally realized being petted felt good. At least once a day she screamed, "It's time for my back rub." Pumpkin became much more social and actually started sneaking downstairs and slinking around the house. But if the doorbell rang, he was faster than Secretariat, disappearing to the safety of my office.

Pearl did venture downstairs once. I wasn't there to see it, but I heard about it from Mark. It was shortly after we moved into our new house. When we made the 300-foot move, my mother brought a can of Spam in case anyone helping carry boxes and furniture needed meat. I'm a vegetarian. Mark wasn't, but he loved vegetarian fare, so we seldom had meat in the house. It was a sad plight for carnivorous cats.

The Spam didn't get eaten, and my mother neglected to take it home. A couple weeks later I had an evening meeting, so Mark was on his own for dinner. He spotted the Spam and decided it was a meat night—if you can call Spam meat.

Slices of the canned loaf were sizzling in the frying pan when Mark heard the loudest meow ever. He turned and saw Pearl—at least he assumed it was Pearl. He traveled a lot and never quite figured out which cat was Pearl and which was Pumpkin.

"It'll be a few minutes before it's done," the chef said to the meat-starved cat.

When the slices were crisp, Mark pulled two plates from the cupboard. He cut Pearl's share into tiny cat-bite sizes and waited for them to cool. He then took both dishes and sat on the kitchen floor, sliding Pearl's plate over to her. She ate the meat, cleaned her face, came to her senses and darted back upstairs.

Pearl and Pumpkin remained elusive, but I learned to appreciate their quirkiness. They always hid when we had guests, which was perfect. The fewer cats seen, the more normal I felt.

Pumpkin and Pearl were inseparable and always slept together.

Rocky, another unwanted young male cat.

Rocky

You might be a crazy cat lady if ... you get calls from friends and family when a stray cat shows up in their yard. You get the same call from distant relatives, neighbors you've never met, friends of friends, and unknown co-workers. On occasion, those same people drop off cats knowing you'll make room for one more.

Rocky moved in on a freezing Saturday in January. Three years earlier we had a new home built behind our farmhouse. The old homestead had a crumbly foundation, a leaky roof with rotting boards, a wet unusable basement and was too small. Despite all its problems, I had a hard time watching my home of 22 years being torn down, loaded into dump trucks and hauled away.

With a spotless, odor-free house, we were particular about which cats could come inside. The sprayers weren't welcome.

Boomer, the white and orange tiger, was living in the new house's attached garage. He had a fluffy cat bed under a heat lamp, a litter box, and food and water bowls. Boomer had been a barn cat, but a young black tomcat who roamed the neighborhood bullied him into retreating to the protection of the garage. Boomer had originally been a house cat but had been evicted when he started spraying. It had been a territorial issue with Smokey, another male cat we had at the time, but their spraying competition earned them a one-way ticket to the barn.

I was heading to Kalamazoo for the day. The last chore before leaving was feeding my horse, Captain. Boomer insisted, like he always did, on making the trek to the barn with me. But this time he refused to return to the garage. I pleaded, bribed him with treats, and tried to get my hands on his scrawny neck.

"You're going to freeze if you stay out here. I'm leaving and won't be back for hours," I told him. He wasn't listening. He was too busy sniffing the floor near the hay, probably enticed by the inviting scent of a mouse. Time was short, so I left him in the barn, with the side door to the garage open. *When he gets cold he'll make his way back to the warmth of his heat lamp*, I thought.

When I returned several hours later, I spotted Boomer in the headlights of the car as he came running from the barn to meet me. That crazy cat. Why didn't he go into the garage?

When I got to the garage, I had my answer. The side door was closed. My first thought was that the wind must have blown it closed, but there had been no wind that day.

I pushed the opener for the overhead door and drove the car in. That's when I spotted him—I did a double take. A cat, glowing like a celestial being, sat under Boomer's heat lamp.

He looked like Boomer, but I was positive I had just seen Boomer outside. The cat was a Boomer look-alike, his stunt double. Instead of orange tiger stripes, the trespasser had tan fur, but his white markings were identical to Boomer's. I got out of the car, expecting the intruder to dodge for the open garage door. He didn't. He stood, lazily stretched, and then jumped out of the bed and sauntered over to Boomer's cat food and started eating.

I was stunned. But as Boomer came running into the garage, I knew enough to grab him before he saw his double. Together we sat in the car and watched the trespasser eat.

What to do? I couldn't kick the newcomer out. It was the depth of winter, during a colder-than-normal stretch of temperatures.

Leaving Boomer in the car, I got out and made sweet talk to the tan cat. He didn't mind my presence. I stroked his back, he purred. Now what? The only option I could see was to bring Boomer into the house. And that's what I did. The inside cats sniffed his butt, followed him as he explored his new surroundings and finally ignored him.

The new cat was so friendly that I knew he belonged to someone. But after placing a found ad in the newspaper and talking to several neighbors, it appeared he was homeless. Another unwanted young cat.

In my questioning, I learned the stray had first appeared at a neighbor's house. They didn't want him, so they took him to another neighbor whose teenager son gladly accepted the feline gift—he was too young to know a cat wasn't a welcomed present. His parents weren't thrilled. They called more neighbors until they hit the people who lived directly across from me. They said, "Janet has a lot of cats. It might be hers."

They brought the unwanted cat to my house, but I wasn't home. What they found was an open side door to the garage. Inside a heat lamp hung above a cat bed, there was a litter box, cat food, but no cat. Problem solved. They put the cat in the garage, closed the door and left.

I didn't have the heart to take the homeless sweetie-pie to the county humane society where adoptions were few and euthanasia was an acceptable form of population control. So I kept him. He became Rocky. After he was neutered and deemed healthy by the vet, I introduced the Boomer-look-alike to the house cats.

So not only was Boomer back in the house, so was his mini-me.

Boomer, left, and his look-alike Rocky.

Rocky.

Buddy and Boots made themselves at
home in the barn.

Buddy the Basketball Cat

You might be a crazy cat lady if ... you quit feeding birds because you realize bird feeders are actually cat feeders.

After Boomer and Rocky transitioned from outside cats to house cats, I decided to do something I'd never done before ... feed birds.

I bought two feeders and hung them on the porch. For the inside cats, I moved chairs to the front windows, providing them with a front row seat to watch the finches, mourning doves, chickadees and woodpeckers stop by to munch on seeds.

Without barn cats, the chipmunk population flourished. The striped rodents also loved birdseed and were soon scavenging under the feeders. Watching the feathered wildlife and other critters eat was pure entertainment for the cats and for me.

But a barn isn't a barn without a cat, and it didn't take long before an orange tabby filled the vacuum. The newcomer mysteriously appeared the day after my husband moved out the first time. I was returning from a walk to the mailbox when the orange tabby strolled out from under a forsythia bush and sat down and announced with a meow, "Here I am."

"What a cutie," I said as I slowly approached him. He didn't move as I stroked his back and tickled his chin.

The tabby seemed a little thin so naturally I offered him a snack. He waited while I went to the house to get the food. "It'll give you energy for your walk home," I told him. He ignored my remark as he crunched the dry nuggets. There was no walk home, only a wait for another free meal.

The tabby was neutered, friendly, confident and so sweet I was sure he belonged to somebody. Unfortunately, that somebody turned out to be me.

The orange cat became Buddy and turned into a faithful companion and confidant. In my sadness and confusion of a marriage falling apart, I'd hang out in the barn to avoid the empty house. Buddy loved being cuddled, never got tired of listening to my woes and always appreciated a hug. He didn't mind my tears as long as they were accompanied by back rubs, sweet talk and food.

But a bowl of cat food on a picnic table in a warm cozy barn is a problem. Actually, it's an invitation. The first time I saw Boots, I didn't even know he was a cat. He was fast, just a blur out of the corner of my eye. It didn't take the stray long to recognize me as a food source. I would see him in the pasture waiting for me to leave so he could come fill his belly.

"Breakfast is here. It's safe. I'm a sucker for cute cats," I'd call to him. It took a couple weeks for him to believe me.

Boots was beautiful. He had a stocky build and was solid

and muscular. He was mostly a gray tabby, but it looked like someone had dipped him in a bucket of white paint: all four feet were white, the tip of his tail matched his toes, and his belly and face were a mismatch of white and tabby.

An early morning sunspot cemented our relationship. One morning when I came out with food, Boots was too warm and comfortable to run. We stared at each other, wondering who would make the next move and what it would be. I decided to ignore him and poured the dry food into the bowl. Buddy started eating. Boots got up, sauntered over and joined him. I petted Buddy and then gently touched Boots. Soon we were friends, and he became a semi-permanent fixture in the barn. It turned out that he belonged to a nearby farm and was boycotting his home due to a new family dog.

With two cats in the barn, chipmunks became scarce. Boots was a master of camouflage and patience. He'd sit in the flowers surrounding the front porch, and his stripes would become one with the black soil. Ground feeders or birds who swooped too low became a meal. To the dismay of the inside cats, I took the bird feeders down.

When cold weather moved in, I hung up two heat lamps for the outside boys—150-watt bulbs above padded cat beds. Within weeks I needed a third. A brown tabby cat, this one a long, lanky female, moved in. Every morning the trio greeted me as I came out of the house and escorted me to their food bowls in the barn.

A few weeks later, Buddy disappeared. I walked the fields and roads calling his name, but there was never an answer. At the time Mark and I were going to counseling.

One evening he stopped by and invited me for a walk at a nearby park. Just as we were finishing our hike, I thought I heard a meow. I stopped and listened. Silence. I called, "Here kitty" and there was an answer. A loud mellow meow, which I recognized.

"It's Buddy," I said. I had told Mark about the missing stray.

"No way! He couldn't be this far from home," Mark said. The park was more than a mile by road from our house. The distance was shorter as the crow flies, but for a cat it would have been a difficult, dangerous walk. Between the park and our home were multiple deep ravines filled with underbrush, trees and predators.

"Buddy, is that you?" I called. A thin orange cat came walking out of the woods straight toward me. I picked him up and recognized his hug. "It's him," I said.

Mark could only stare in disbelief. Buddy sat on my lap the whole drive home. I carried him to the picnic table and he ate and ate. Buddy never left home after that. Actually, I don't think he ever strayed farther from the barn than to meet me at the house as I took food to him. While the other barn cats went for walks and would be gone for a few hours, Buddy was always there ... eating. That's when he started to inflate and became Buddy, the basketball cat.

Sweet Buddy.

Izzy's one and only litter of kittens.

Six Black Kittens

You might be a crazy cat lady if ... you have two or more black cats and you love Halloween because stores are full of black-cat decorations.

I counted once. I counted twice. After I counted six the third time, I assumed my counting skills were intact. The brown tabby cat had delivered babies in my barn in a fuzzy, pink kitty bed under a 150-watt heat lamp. I admit I pamper my outside cats, but Michigan winters are whisker-freezing cold. The heap of newborns bore little resemblance to kittens. At first I thought the pile of fur was a batch of mice or moles. But Mom Cat's thin physique was a major clue: the bulge was gone.

"Why are all your babies black?" I asked the brown tabby. Izzy had been a barn cat down the road, but after she discovered the heat lamps hanging from the rafters in my barn, she decided to stay for the winter.

I thought of the dancing Lipizzaner stallions and recalled how they were born black and turned white as they aged. Maybe the babies would grow into calicos or tabbies. My knowledge of kittens was nil—all my cats were spayed or neutered before they had a chance at loving.

I couldn't leave the baby furry-balls in the garage. I feared they'd become a raccoon snack or, even worse, roast under the scorching bulb since they didn't have the motor skills to escape. So, while Mom Cat nursed her brood, I picked up the pink kitty bed and carried the precious cargo into the house.

"You'll be safer in the house," I said as I struggled with the awkward load. Mama didn't flinch; I think the move was part of her master plan.

I deposited the new family in the master bedroom. Mark and I had separated eight months earlier, and I was sleeping in the guest room.

I absolutely loved being the human mom to Izzy's babies. I marveled at her patience, at her attentiveness as she cleaned each one with soothing licks.

Boring is what the kittens were the first few days. They squirmed, they lined up to nurse and they slept. Eat and sleep, just like human babies. It didn't take them long to outgrow the pink bed. I cut down the sides of a large cardboard box to four inches, put in flowered towels and moved the family into their new digs.

One of the babies inherited Izzy's polydactyl feet—she had an extra toe on each foot. Her big feet spawned the name Little Baby Big Foot. She was also the only one to have a few white hairs on her chest, which weren't as noteworthy in the naming process. I couldn't tell the other kittens apart, so they didn't get individual names. Collectively they were The Babies.

When they were about a week old, they opened their eyes, which were brilliant blue, a beautiful contrast to their black fur.

The Babies wobbled on shaky legs in a world limited by cardboard walls. There was a string of firsts: The first time they left the box, the first time they used me as a jungle gym, their claws scaling up my back to perch on my shoulders like parrots, the first time they purred.

One of the most exciting firsts was the discovery of the litter box. They dug like little archeologists in search of Egyptian treasures. But instead of plundering, they left surprises for me: marble-size clumps of pee and little-bitty Tootsie Rolls. Exciting stuff.

The Babies had endless energy. They raced around the room like a herd of wild horses. They attacked stuffed toys and played hide-and-seek in an upside down cardboard box with kitten-size holes cut into its sides. Their rough-and-tumble play usually resulted in piercing squeals of pain, and I became a referee, stepping in and calling time-out.

"Play nice," I'd say. Their energy would dwindle, and one by one they'd lose steam and find a place to rest. Soon they'd all be sleeping in their signature heap.

"Appreciate your babies," I told Mom Cat. "They're going to be the last ones you have." She would be spayed when the kittens were weaned.

The only things that changed color as The Babies grew were their eyes. The kittens remained black, but their blue eyes transformed to emerald green. Their coloring was worrisome. Black cats are often objects of superstition with people considering them bad luck. Black cats are also associated with witchcraft and are an iconic symbol of Halloween cats with their arched backs and glowing eyes.

In reality, bad luck goes to the cat who is born black. Talk to anyone who works in a shelter or rescue and they will tell you black kittens are the last to get adopted, if they get adopted at all. People want calicos, Siamese, tabbies, tuxedo cats and cats with odd markings and coloring.

I was tempted to keep all six kittens, but Mark said no. Since we were going to counseling to get our marriage back on track, I was trying to make him happy. I contacted the director of a rescue group where I volunteered, and she was willing to take the cats into their adoption program as long as I provided them a foster home. No problem.

The Babies passed their feline leukemia tests, got their first vaccines and were spayed or neutered. They also got individual names. The boys became Tex, Domino and Decker and the girls were Imelda, Sweetie and Little Big Foot. On adoption day they wore colored collars made of orange ribbon with their name written in black. Not being able to tell them apart was a blessing for me—I didn't know them as individuals, except for Little Baby Big Foot. This made it easier to say good-bye.

I prayed the kittens would find forever homes, because the only thing harder to adopt out than a black kitten is an adult black cat. This point was driven home for me when I was working on an article about cats used in dissection in high schools. One student said most of the cats brought in for dissection were black. Why? Because black cats don't get adopted, and some shelters sell the bodies of the cats they euthanize to biological companies who, in turn, prep them and sell them for dissection.

It was tough taking The Babies to adoption day. How do you part with family? The bad news was that none of them got adopted. The good news was that none of them got adopted.

It was decided three of them—Tex, Domino and Imelda— could stay at the store until they found homes. I cried all the way home with Decker, Sweetie and Baby Big Foot.

Domino was the first to get a new home, leaving room for another one in the cage. Decker went. By then I couldn't take it any more. I paid the adoption fees, which covered the vet bills, and Sweetie and Baby Big Foot were mine.

I visited the three kittens at the pet store so often that the employees all knew me. Soon Tex was gone, then Imelda. Decker was alone for a couple weeks, but he was a trooper. The woman in charge of adoptions worried that he had been caged too long and asked if I would bring him home to give him a break.

Yes! I knew if I got Decker home, he would never leave again. I was to go pick him up the next day. But before I left, she called again and said someone had filled out an application for him. A little later she called once more and said, "Good news! The application was approved," and Decker was gone.

Baby Big Foot grew and needed a more dignified name. Her constant habit of stretching inspired another silly name: Stretch.

When Stretch and Sweetie are going crazy and tearing up the house, I often see six instead of two, and I wonder what life would be like if I had kept the whole family.

If I had known then what I learned later, Mark would have been neutered and put in a cage at the pet store, and I would have kept all six babies.

Izzy, aka Mom cat, with her babies.

Sweetie and Stretch.

Ernie, the only survivor from a litter of barn kittens.

Ernie, Ernesto and Emma

You might be a crazy cat lady if ... you can't say no when someone asks if you can provide a foster home for kittens.

My thoughts bombarded me like freezing rain on a windshield. Could I do it again? Could I foster kittens and then give them up for adoption? The black kittens were one of the most wonderful, and yet one of the most heartbreaking experiences of my life.

Heather, an animal rescue volunteer, had dropped off dog food at a local animal shelter, and the young woman in the office was distressed. Someone had brought in barn kittens whose mother had disappeared. Two babes from the litter of five had already died. The remaining little guys needed special care, and the shelter wasn't equipped to give it. The woman saw Heather as a solution.

Heather called the rescue's president and was advised to walk away. The struggling rescue had too many cats and not enough foster homes. I wasn't surprised to hear that Heather ignored the advice and took the kittens. Heather loved animals and had a big heart, but she also had a husband, a full-time job, and a house full of cats and dogs. It was impossible for her to keep the babies.

The kittens weren't newborns. Their eyes were open, and they were able to eat on their own, but they were starving and probably dehydrated and in need of human attention to socialize them.

Heather called and asked if I could take them. I said yes. We arranged to meet the next day for the hand-off. There were only two kittens when we met. Heather was almost in tears as she explained how one didn't survive the night. The other two were tucked in a blanket inside a cat carrier. She noted one was a bit stronger than the other but both had eaten that morning. She said they were both boys.

When I got home I put them under a heat lamp in the spare bedroom. One was a gray tiger and the other a mix of calico and stripes. Both had extra toes like Little Big Foot, aka Stretch, and Mom Cat. I gave them water and canned kitten food. They both ate.

But in the morning the tiger was wobbling around the room while his brother appeared listless. I tried to coax him to eat, tried teasing him into drinking. He wasn't interested. He was shutting down. Soon he was motionless with just a vague rise and fall of his side as his lungs struggled to bring air to his system. His brother stayed close. He was dying, and I knew it. I held him for a while and told him he was loved. I was helpless. Later, when I returned, he was gone, and his brother was cuddled with his small body. I left them alone. A couple hours later, I removed the tiny body and buried it. It was the smallest grave I ever had to dig.

The striped guy took his brother's death in stride. I felt

bad for him to be an only child, but it didn't seem to bother him. When I was sure he was going to survive, I started searching for a name. I settled on Ernie, after the author Ernest Hemingway, who owned cats with extra toes.

Somewhere along the line, Ernie evolved into Ernesto. Maybe it was a bit more dignified. He answered to both. I bought him a bag of Purina Kitten Chow, and he loved to lap up the gravy when I poured warm water over the crunchy dry food. He thrived.

I would watch television with him, and it didn't take him long to figure out how to climb onto the bed. The extra toes gave extra climbing power. He'd attack my feet under the blanket and leap on my face when I least expected it. He was all kitten, and I wanted to keep him, but Mark said no. Ernesto was a male and our experience with male cats could be summed up in one word: spray. They all seemed to feel a need to mark their territory, despite the fact that they were all neutered. Boomer had been evicted to the barn, so had Rocky. Pumpkin was the only male house cat, and he liked it that way. Ernesto had to go.

Safe Haven did adoptions the last two Saturdays of every month at a local pet supply store. It was early December, and Ernie wasn't old enough to be vaccinated and neutered in time for a pre-Christmas adoption date. So I took a cute picture of him and wrote a heart-felt story of his young life, adding that he would be available for adoption shortly.

A woman saw the flyer and was interested. Her daughter desperately wanted a kitten, a gray tiger kitten to be exact, and they had been looking for the perfect kitten for months.

She called and asked to come visit Ernesto without her daughter. Ernesto greeted her with all his charm and then was off playing with Stretch and Sweetie. The woman liked him. Would he be available before Christmas? Could I pretend to be Santa's helper and deliver him Christmas Eve? I said yes, but my heart said no.

Ernesto fit into our house like he was meant to be there. I desperately wanted to call and say I had changed my mind, but Mark said no—somewhere there was a little girl who wanted a kitten for Christmas, and her mom was expecting Santa to deliver.

Taking Ernesto to get neutered started as a typical trip to the veterinarian. He was weighed and checked in, and I was told to call that afternoon to see when he'd be ready to come home. I called and got the shock of my life, much like the one the vet got when he went to perform the surgery.

Ernesto wasn't a boy. He was a girl. Heather had said the kitten was a boy and I never checked. Gone was the worry of his developing a need to spray. But there was the promise. I called the woman and told her of the mistake, that Ernie was a girl. I prayed the news would make her change her mind. I recalled her saying she had been looking for a male cat, that female cats weren't as friendly. But she didn't hesitate; she said she was sure Ernie was still the cat for them.

On Christmas Eve I told Stretch and Sweetie to say good-bye. I loaded Ernie into a carrier for the trip to her new home. She cried. Mark drove so I was able to take her out of the carrier. I held her and she still cried. My heart ached.

We found the street, and then the house, and we walked

up the sidewalk and rang the doorbell. My voice broke as I tried to tell my tale of being Santa's helper. Finally I just held out the carrier. The little girl was surprised. She opened the carrier door and Ernie dodged out. Within seconds the girl and her younger brother were in pursuit. I noticed a Christmas tree and told myself *Ernie will love climbing that.* The woman invited me to visit any time. We left. I cried. It spoiled the holiday, which turned out to be my last Christmas with Mark.

About a month later, I went back to visit Ernie. Because of her change in sex, they decided she needed a new name and settled on Emma. Emma had been declawed shortly before my visit and was still not understanding why she couldn't climb. I called her and she ignored me. I finally grabbed her, held her tight and stared into her eyes. There was no hint of recognition. Had she forgotten me in such a short span of time or was she mad at me? Mad for giving her away, mad because she was an only cat with no big sisters to play with, mad because she could no longer climb.

Two months later, Mark moved out and filed for a divorce. My world crumbled. I was devastated, angry and alone. Looking back, I wish he would have left before insisting I couldn't keep Ernie.

Kirby after he recuperated and was up for adoption.

Kirby: A Lesson in Ringworm

You might be a crazy cat lady if ... you were horrified the first time you heard the word ringworm, but now it doesn't faze you.

He looked like an old man in need of Rogain. Kirby, a foster cat with Safe Haven Humane Society, had thinning black hair, a blank stare and a skin rash making him unfit for adoption. He had been to the vet a few times and put on various medications, but none of them worked. His foster mom was going on a two-week cruise, and she asked if I would take him into my home.

"I promise you he doesn't have anything contagious," she assured me.

I didn't hesitate to say yes. Eileen was one of the most dedicated, caring women I had ever met. I felt honored that she would trust me with her special-needs cat.

"No problem," I said. "He can have the guest room. I'm not planning on company."

Two weeks later Eileen delivered Kirby. I led her to the back bedroom. She set Kirby's carrier on the floor and opened the door. He slowly emerged. As he investigated his new home, Eileen handed me a bag of cat food, medication and instructions.

"You need to smash a half pill and thoroughly mix it into a quarter can of cat food. If it's not ground as fine as possible, he'll eat around it."

She gave Kirby good-bye kisses.

"Don't worry, I'll take good care of him," I said as I walked her to the door.

"I'll call when I get back."

After she left, I returned to the bedroom. The house cats wanted in, but I told them our guest preferred to be alone. "Give him a few days and maybe he'll be up to visitors."

Kirby was sniffing every square inch of the room. I sat on the bed and watched. He was coal black ... where he had hair. I scooped him up and plopped him onto the bed.

"It's you and me for two weeks," I said. I scratched his head. There were little bumps all over his skin. If Eileen hadn't assured me he didn't have anything contagious, I would have worried.

She was right about him smelling his medication. It became a no-win game of trying to persuade him to eat. He knew when there was medicine in the food. "I'm not trying to poison you," I'd say as I coaxed him to eat. I finally gave up and began shoving the pill down his throat before he had time to react. It didn't take him long to catch on and his jaws locked in place like vise grips whenever I came near.

I tried to convince him I was a friend. I brushed him and petted his bumpy skin every afternoon as we watched Oprah. Never once did he purr, and his skin condition only got worse. When Eileen finally came home, I felt terrible telling her that he wasn't doing the best. She came right over. I ushered her into his room and opened the door. She took one look at him and put her hands to her face. "He has ringworm," she whispered.

"Ringworm?" I repeated. I wasn't familiar with ringworm, and I didn't like the sound of it.

"He was exposed to it months ago. He's been tested twice and both times the results were negative."

"Don't worry about it." I tried to remain calm.

"I'm so sorry," she kept saying.

She explained the condition had nothing to do with worms but was a fungus. It was highly contagious.

"Did your cats have contact with him?" she asked. They hadn't. She was relieved. She said she'd ask her vet if there was anything I should do.

She called the next day and said I should spray diluted bleach water around the room. *Would I be able to have company in that room again?* She added that the vet said the ringworm had been inactive and the stress of being in a new place probably brought on the symptoms.

Eileen apologized repeatedly. She mailed me medication for my cats and told me to watch for round rings with indented centers, which is where the fungus got its name.

Every day I checked each cat. Every day I was relieved to find smooth skin.

About two weeks later I noticed my neck had red spots. I felt them and was horrified to feel a round ring with no center. I frantically called Eileen.

"Yes, people can catch it," she said. "I'm so sorry."

I recalled hugging Kirby, his face cuddled into my neck.

I called my doctor and talked to a nurse who said if it was ringworm, all I had to do was go to the store and buy an over-the-counter anti-fungal cream for athlete's foot. If it didn't start to clear up in a week, I was to call back.

I went online and found the miracle cure for ringworm— $49.50 for a one-ounce bottle, plus $29.95 for overnight shipping. Guaranteed to clear it up in two days. I refused to pay the price. Instead, I started wearing turtlenecks.

Unfortunately, I was cat-sitting for a neighbor's three cats while the family spent the winter months in Florida. Every day I'd walk the half-mile to their house and watch a little television with the kitties. They were so lonely they'd fight over who got my lap and take turns cuddling with me on the couch.

The next day I noticed bumpy spots on one of them. I called their vet, but she refused to treat the cats without permission from their owner.

"But I don't want to tell them I gave their cats ringworm," I pleaded. In the end, I made the call. My neighbor, who was due home shortly, said he'd take care of his cats when he got there. Like Eileen, I apologized until he told me to quit.
But the next fall he didn't call to ask me to cat-sit. So I called him. "Did I lose my cat-sitting job due to the ringworm?" He laughed. "No, we're not going to Florida this year."

Sad little Geo Cat.

Geo Cat

You might be a crazy cat lady if ... kittens and cats appear out of nowhere and land on your porch, in your barn and in your yard.

I seldom say no to an invitation to go geocaching. In case you don't know, geocaching is a high-tech version of hide-and-seek. Players hide a container with items for trade and a logbook and leave the coordinates for the treasures on a website. Anyone can enter the coordinates into a hand-held GPS (global positioning system) unit or into an app on their smart phone and the hunt is on.

Before I could leave for the evening's fun with my niece, I had to feed my horse. A scoop of grain and he'd be set. Little did I know what was waiting for me in a sunspot outside the barn door: a gray tabby kitten. He was a friendly little guy, making himself right at home with the other barn cats. He purred when I stroked his back. I asked him not to be there when I returned.

"I already have eight cats. I don't need nine," I told him.

Yellow eyes glowed in the headlights of my car when I pulled in the driveway a few hours later. He was waiting for me. I secretly hoped he would be.

Melissa and I had brainstormed names for the stray while hiking the woods in search of a well-hidden cache. We stumbled upon the treasure-filled ammo box hidden under a pile of logs about the same time we stumbled upon a name: Geo Cat.

The next morning Geo was waiting for breakfast with the rest of the gang. Determined not to add another cat to my collection, I emailed a friend who ran an adoption program. If I could foster Geo Cat, she could find him a home, but first he had to be tested for feline leukemia, neutered and vaccinated. No problem, but that's when Geo became a house cat and started to worm his way into my life.

Adoption Day

At PetSmart I fixed up Geo's cage with a towel, cat bed, litter box, food and water. I deposited him onto the bed, wrote his brief history on a card that hung on the cage door and said good-by. He didn't say a word.

Six hours later I returned, my heart pounding. Would Geo be gone? He wasn't. He was in the same position I had left him, food untouched, and not a grain of litter out of place.

A young couple sat at a table filling out an adoption application. "Who are you adopting?" I asked. "The gray tabby kitten is my foster."

"We looked at him, but he seemed lifeless," the woman said.

"Lifeless? He's a bundle of energy." I wished them luck with their new cat and went to check on Geo. He pretended not to recognize me. I opened the cage door and picked him up. He hung in my arms like a beanie-bag cat.

"What's the matter?" I asked. He didn't answer. He didn't move. He was indeed lifeless. The adopt-a-thon was done, so I loaded the limp little guy into a carrier and the carrier into the car. Geo didn't say a word all the way home.

I carried the carrier into the house and sat it on the kitchen floor. I opened its door, and Geo poked out his head. Stretch and Sweetie watched from the living room—they were Geo's favorite cats to torment. When he spotted the one-year-old sisters, he was off running. He chased them to the basement and a minute later the three came running back up the stairs, this time with Geo in the lead. After a couple laps around the living room, Geo stopped and called a time-out. He trotted to the food bowl and ate like he hadn't eaten all day—and he hadn't. Then he drank like he hadn't drunk all day—and he hadn't. Then he was off running with Sweetie and Stretch in pursuit. Geo was home.

I didn't say a word.

Cat Number Nine

As I write this, Geo Cat is sprawled on my desk watching the computer cursor with the intent of a cat stalking a spider. He paws the screen but gets bored with the flat surface. He swats my graduation tassel hanging from the desk lamp, and then attacks the tiny knickknack cats cluttering the base of the monitor. "Will you please stop?" I ask. He settles down for a snooze on the stacks of papers cluttering my workspace.

After witnessing Geo's depression on adoption day, I didn't have the heart to take him back to the store again. I paid his adoption fee, which covered the expense of the vet visit, and he was officially cat number nine.

Later, I realized his melancholy performance on adoption day was the same as when I first had brought him into the house and quarantined him in the guest room. I attributed his low energy to being hungry and tired. Looking back, I think he was sad. I think he missed a life that most likely included his mamma and littermates. He was used to people, so, somewhere, somebody had given him love and attention, but apparently not enough to prevent the person from dropping him off in my barn.

After a couple days of being in the bedroom, Geo snapped out of his depression. Maybe it was when he discovered the guestroom bathroom, specifically the toilet paper. He unrolled an entire roll. I left the heap of Northern with a shake of my head and thoughts of picking it up when I had more time. An hour later the heap was tattered confetti throughout both rooms. It clogged the vacuum.

Soon Geo had the run of the entire house, and it didn't take him long to discover another bathroom. The toilet paper game was repeated, but this time I cleaned up immediately. From then on, the toilet paper was kept on the counter. But then Geo discovered jumping and with jumping discovered the toilet paper. Bits of paper littered the whole house. I

cleaned up after his private party but couldn't find the roll. Every day when I wasn't around, he'd play with his toilet paper, and I'd come home to shredded ribbons of tissue. The game got old, and I searched till I found his stash hidden under a bed. From then on, the toilet paper was kept in a drawer. I work hard to remember to remind guests of its location.

Hobbies and Obsessions

Geo definitely had a paper fetish. At first I thought it was just a toilet paper obsession, but the fixation extended to paper towels, gift-wrapping and Kleenex. During the holiday season, I left red tissue paper on the kitchen counter with the intent of stuffing gift bags the next day. Geo beat me to it. In the morning I was greeted by shredded red tissue paper littering the floor, and the guilty party was innocently waiting for breakfast.

Geo also loved pulling tissues from their box and ripping them into tiny pieces. Tissue boxes were then kept upside down.

"What will people think when the toilet paper is in a drawer and the Kleenex boxes are upside down?" I ask Geo. *That you don't know what fun is*, I imagine him saying.

Another hobby Geo has taken to is what I call screening. It's a cat version of rock climbing. When it's hot and the sliding glass door is open, he gets a running start, leaps, and then claws his way up the screen. Geo is bummed when the door is closed. But then he discovered the skylights in the angled walls of my office where the screens are on the inside. A shelf under the windows, meant for plants, is the perfect place for Geo to start his ascent. The slanted screens are a challenge and often leave him dangling mid-air from front claws.

Geo is also an amateur soccer player. During the night he sneaks onto the kitchen counter and knocks to the floor whatever he finds: ink pens, a wad of tinfoil meant for recycling or a roll of film ready for developing. He bats the object across the vinyl floor like a hockey puck. If the counters are clean, Geo has a fallback plan. He leaps at the refrigerator door and knocks off the magnetic chip-clips and cat magnets.

Kitten Fun

Every morning I clean litter boxes: one upstairs, two

downstairs using plastic grocery bags for disposal. I got sidetracked one morning and left the bag with its clumps of litter-coated pee and poop on the floor while I did a quick check of email. Geo Cat discovered the bag and was intently sniffing its contents when I spotted him from across the room.

"Geo, leave it alone," I said calmly.

His head came out of the bag with one of the handles looped around his neck. Before I could move, he panicked and ran down the stairs with the bag in close pursuit. Used litter spilled everywhere as Geo tried to outrun the plastic demon. By the time I made it down the stairs, all was quiet, and Geo was nowhere to be seen.

"Geo," I called in my least threatening voice. "Where are you?" I worried he was strangling in plastic.

I finally found him squashed beneath the entertainment center. I reached my hand under it and was able to grab the bag. The plastic stretched and ripped. I pulled it out. It was completely empty. A couple minutes later Geo crawled out, dusted himself off and calmly walked away—tiptoeing among the clumps of litter.

"Are you going to help clean this mess?" He ignored me.

Sweet Gee

Despite his love for destructive fun, there's a ton of sweetness and unbiased attitude in Geo. He'll play with anybody, and he loves to snuggle. Some of the older, set-in-their-way cats stare with disgust at his antics, but they accept his intruding presence. Even scaredy-cat Pearl has been known to cuddle with Geo for a snooze. A winter with record-high heating bills and lowered thermostats helps with the cuddle factor.

Geo's nickname is Gee; it rolls off the tongue much easier than Geo. His tail salutes to a 90-degree angle when I say either of his names as he saunters through a room. He often detours to my lap. I admire his gray fur with its charcoal tiger stripes, his belly a soft pastel gray with random dark spots. I tease him, saying I'm pushing his buttons as I poke the spots on his plump underside. Sometimes he likes it, sometimes he tolerates it, and sometimes he leaves.

I often tell him his fur would make a beautiful coat or maybe matching trim on hood and gloves. I tell him he's lucky he's not a Chinese cat where they raise cats and dogs for their fur. He ignores me. He knows he's safe in my house.

Geo Cat playing with magnets on the refrigerator.

Above: Wild Cat before he was tamed.
Below: Stretch telling Wild Cat a secret.

Wild Cat, I Think You Love Me

You might be a crazy cat lady if ... you spend a year taming a feral cat.

Wild Cat bounced off the walls of the exam room in a desperate search for an escape. He leaped onto a shelf packed with supplies. His added weight pulled the anchors from the drywall, and the shelf with Wild Cat and its collection of boxes and bottles crashed to the floor.

The fall didn't slow Wild Cat. He ping-ponged in circles around me and the veterinarian technician who was trying to catch him. She hadn't listened when I said the brown tabby was wild. She thought she was going to open the dog kennel, grab him and move him to a cat carrier. When she opened the kennel door, Wild Cat, who had probably been planning an escape for the duration of his captivity, slid past her before she knew he was moving.

Wild Cat's story began a few months earlier. Like cats do, he appeared out of nowhere, moved into the barn and assumed he was the sole proprietor. The quiet of the farm erupted with fights as the barn cats tried to defend their turf. It wasn't long before I was taking Mom Cat and Buddy to the vet to have infected wounds tended.

It was Buddy's first visit to the vet, and Dr. Dawn commented on his weight. "He's a couch potato," she said. "It happens sometimes when male cats are neutered."

"He's a barn cat," I said. I felt bad that Buddy didn't have a couch to be a potato on.

Both cats needed antibiotics. I took them home, confined them to the basement and tended their injuries twice daily. The house cats were kept upstairs.

Back in the barn, Wild Cat ruled. Boots no longer came around and Rocky hid in the woods. That's when I borrowed a live trap. I set it during the day, not wanting to catch any nocturnal skunks, raccoons or opossums. On day two, Wild Cat was mine.

"What a pretty kitty," I said as I approached the trap. He lunged and spit at me. I was thankful he was caged. I carried the trap into the garage and butted it against a large dog kennel. I opened the trap's door and Wild Cat dodged into the larger prison. He was confined for a week before his appointment to get neutered.

"Let's hope the surgery takes away a little of your aggression," I said as I loaded the blanket-covered dog kennel into my vehicle. He hissed and growled.

The technician was finally successful in catching Wild Cat. "Come back tomorrow afternoon and he'll be ready to go home," she said. The next day Wild Cat was quiet, but it was only the effect of the drugs.

"It'll take a few weeks, maybe a couple months, before the testosterone is out of his system," she said.

For 15 days I kept Wild Cat in the dog kennel. There was no befriending him. He hissed, he growled and he continued to lunge at me. The only way I could clean his litter box and give him fresh water and food was to put long sticks in the slots of the kennel and confine him to the back half of the cage.

"You're a handsome guy. I'm not going to hurt you," I'd say in a non-threatening monotone.

He apparently didn't believe a word I said.

Wild Cat never ate, drank or used the litter during the day, but every morning his cage would be a disaster. Food scattered, water spilled and the litter box moved and well used. The blanket, covering the back half of the cage to give the prisoner a place to hide, would be partially pulled through the openings of the wire-mesh kennel and tattered.

I felt sorry for Wild Cat. The day came when I realized I wasn't making any progress in taming him. I opened the garage door and watched as he sniffed the fresh air. I opened the kennel door and stepped back. It took him a few seconds to react. Then he was gone. He ran so fast I thought I'd never see him again.

After Mom Cat and Buddy healed, they went back to the barn. Rocky came out of hiding. Life was peaceful until the weather started to turn cold. Wild Cat returned and so did the fights. He discovered one of the heat lamps that hung from the barn rafters, and I knew he wasn't going anywhere until spring.

Mom Cat disappeared, and I brought Buddy back into the house, this time introducing him to the house cats. After sniffing butts they were accepting of one another.

"You can be a real couch potato," I told him. He became a *double coucher*. During the day he snoozed on the sofa in my office. During the evening hours he slept on the couch in the living room.

Before I could get Rocky into the house, he disappeared.

I debated if I should unplug the last heat lamp and quit taking food to the barn for Wild Cat, but I couldn't do it despite the trouble he caused. My appaloosa had died in September and, without a horse to tend to, I had no reason to go to the barn every day. Still I couldn't desert the elusive tabby who always hid from me. The only reason I knew he was still around was because the food was eaten.

I discovered that if I didn't slam the house door when I headed for the barn, and tiptoed across the snow-covered lawn, I could catch a glimpse of Wild Cat through a window as he basked in the warmth of the heat lamp. By the time I made my way around to the door, he would be gone.

"Wild Cat, I know you're here. I brought breakfast," I'd say as I poured the dry kibbles as loudly as I could into the bowl. I knew he was hiding in the hay. It took a few weeks before he would answer my sweet talk, and then it was with low, deep growls. Over the next few weeks the growl evolved into faint meows. Then came the day when his head popped up from behind a bale of hay.

"There you are. Come down here and eat." He'd dodge back into hiding until I was gone, but as time passed he slowly revealed more of himself.

"Come down here and I'll scratch your back." The bribe didn't work. He listened as he sat on top of the stack of hay. Soon he was rolling around on his back and rubbing his face against the corner of the bales. He wanted to be scratched as much I wanted to rub his itches. "You're going to be domesticated yet," I teased.

We stayed at that social level for weeks. Wild Cat strutting, rolling around and rubbing himself against the bales; me coaxing him to come closer. Finally he was close enough for me to hold out my hand to him. I thought he would sniff it. Instead he swatted and drew blood. From then on I wore heavy gloves.

The day I touched his head we both panicked. I pulled back and he ran. Within a week of the first touch, I could pet him, but only if he was on a certain bale of hay. It was his safety zone, his home plate.

By spring, he had worked up the nerve to come near me in the yard as I tended the flower gardens. He'd roll in the grass begging for attention. When I'd reach to touch him, he'd jump to his feet and run for the barn. He'd stop after a few feet to see if I was following. If I followed, he'd lead me to his bale of hay. If I ignored him, he'd come closer and roll around on his back again. It was a tiring game.

It was midsummer when Wild Cat discovered the back deck with its sliding glass door where he could peer into the house. It became his summer home and, instead of hiking daily to the barn with his meals, I began placing them on the deck.

The inside cats didn't appreciate the outside visitor. They growled and tried to attack through the glass, but Wild Cat ignored their intimidation tactics. I remember the first time I left the sliding glass door open, leaving only the screen to protect Wild Cat from the house gang. Both sides took a step back. There was sniffing, growling and finally acceptance.

I realized Wild Cat was pleased with his summer digs when he started bringing me gifts. I love gifts, but Wild Cat made poor choices for this vegetarian cat-lover. There were decapitated mice, blood-oozing chipmunks and once a matching pair of baby black squirrels. I removed them with my eyes mostly closed. Procrastination proved to be a savior. If I left the dead bodies overnight, by morning they would be gone. I finally caught an opossum scavenging on the deck for midnight treats, and the mystery of the disappearing corpses was solved.

When summer eased into autumn and the mornings were tinged with frost, I started carrying Wild Cat's food to the barn again. He followed me to the barn and then followed me back to the house.

"Your breakfast is on the picnic table in the barn," I told him. The days of the open, sliding glass door were long gone, and I felt a tinge of guilt as he sat outside watching our every move. The guilt was really heavy when I flipped on the gas fireplace and the inside cats (and I) basked in its warmth.

"Go to the barn," became my mantra. Wild Cat ignored me. Then came an early snow in October. Big fluffy flakes drifted from the sky and started to turn the outside world white. Wild Cat curled into a ball in the corner of the deck. I couldn't take it. I opened the slider and screen door.

"Wild Cat, do you want to be a house cat?"

It was the invitation he had been waiting for. He strutted into the house like it was something he did every day. As he inspected the layout, the inside cats trailed him, taking turns sniffing his butt. He ignored them. The summer of only having a screen door separating them made the transition easy.

Two months later, Wild Cat was attacking catnip toys, snoozing by the fireplace, and chasing and being chased in play with the younger generation of house cats. He slept on my bed and insisted on cuddling close.

Wild Cat's trust in me evolved into a trust of everyone. He greeted all who came into the house, be it family, friend or repairman. Whenever the doorbell rang, all the cats would run and hide except Wild Cat and Stretch—these two ran to the door to see who was there.

"Not everyone is as nice to cats as I am," I warned him. He listened, but he knew any friend of mine was a friend of his.

An older Rocky after talking his way
back into the house.

Rocky, in the House Again

You might be a crazy cat lady if ... you can't stop cats from weaseling their way into your heart and home.

When Wild Cat first appeared, he terrorized all the barn cats. Boots was the first to disappear—I never saw him again. Then Mom Cat was gone. I assumed they returned to their farm. Rocky disappeared in December.

I was concerned for Buddy's safety and feared he'd go missing too. He was the last barn cat, except for the invading tomcat. What choice did I have but to bring Buddy into the house? He didn't object to being carried from barn to house. I made him comfortable in the guest room and, after a few days of confinement, formally introduced him to the other house cats. He fit right in. He was a Buddy to everyone.

I checked the barn several times a day hoping Rocky would return. After a week, I thought the odds of surviving the cold weather were against him, but I was wrong. He was gone two weeks before he came home. I heard his meow and saw his face peering into the sidelight window of the front door.

"Where have you been?" I asked as I opened the door. He

answered in a wispy, sore-throat meow. He was skinny, dirty and limping.

I picked him up; he was a featherweight. Just bones covered with skin. I carried him to the guest room, recently vacated by Buddy. I gave him dry food, water and opened a can of his favorite wet food: turkey and cheese in gravy. He devoured it all. I held him.

"Where have you been?" I asked. He purred, his voice raspy. In addition to being dirty, he had a stale smell.

A light snow had fallen the night before Rocky came home. When I went outside later that day, I saw his tracks on the sidewalk in front of the house. They came from the south side of the house. I followed the little paw prints. They went through thickets of wild roses and thorn trees, up and down two ravines and meandered across a hayfield. The trail led to a vacant farm and into a pole barn. I walked around the structure and picked up his tracks on the other side. They soon disappeared into an old wooden barn, but they came out the other side. I lost the trail at the road, which had been recently plowed.

Maybe Rocky had been accidentally locked in someone's outbuilding across the street. Or maybe he had been living in the barns. I wish he could tell his tale. It took a few weeks for his ribs to disappear and the sheen to come back to his coat. After he recuperated, he, too, became a house cat.

Rocky, left, and Buddy became best friends.

Frosty, a foster kitten who never left.

Frosty the Flake

You might be a crazy cat lady if ... you adopt kittens you're supposed to be fostering.

Not long after the foster kitten was named Frosty, she earned the nickname of *Frosty Flake*. The three-month-old had flaky behaviors: she ran almost non-stop, she wiggled and squirmed when held, she seldom purred, and she squeezed under the dresser whenever she felt threatened, making it almost impossible to catch her.

Frosty was one of several kittens taken from a hoarding case that included 55 cats. I'm not usually asked to foster (I get too attached), but this was an emergency: the humane society I volunteered for didn't have enough foster homes. So my spare bedroom became a temporary home to four of the babies.

Frosty was a dilute torti: dark gray with streaks of cream. Her face looked like she'd gotten her head caught in a can of butter-cream frosting.

"Torti" is short for tortoiseshell, which is not a breed but a coloring. A traditional torti is a mix of black and brown with hints of orange. A dilute torti has a dilute gene, which softens the colors. The black becomes gray and the orange becomes cream.

Frosty had a toy called Cat Dancer—a two-foot long piece of spring wire with a small twist of cardboard on each end. She leaped, pounced, and chased the slip of cardboard like a cat after a bug. The best way to catch Frosty was to get her focused on chasing the fake prey. When she got close to me, I'd scoop her up. She didn't appreciate being captured.

After a vet check and spay/neuter surgeries, my guests were ready for the next step in finding their permanent homes. There was an opening at a local pet supply store that allowed rescue groups to display felines in need of homes. All four of my fosters were put into one cage, and I left knowing the kittens would quickly find homes. They were young, had beautiful markings and were quite personable ... except for Frosty's quirkiness.

Callie was the first to get adopted, but before the others could sweet-talk their way into someone's life, Frosty got the sniffles and a runny nose. All three had to come back to my spare room, and Frosty was put on antibiotics.

"Did you get sick just so you could come back here?" I asked her. She ran and dodged under the dresser and refused to come out. Giving her antibiotics twice daily didn't endear me to the feisty little feline.

By the time she felt better, there was no longer room for the trio at the pet store, so I had to keep them two more weeks. When space finally became available, the kittens had grown and couldn't fit in one cage. Only two could go. I kept Frosty. After one kitten was adopted, it was Frosty's turn to go. She was terrified when I pulled her from the cat carrier and put her in the cage. It took her a minute to recognize her friend Gracie, and the two of them huddled together. It broke my heart.

In a few days, I got an email saying someone had fallen in love with Gracie and she was going to her new home. Poor Frosty. She'd be alone.

Then came a second email; Frosty was being a curmudgeon. She was hissing at people who wanted to pet her, and no one would adopt a kitten who wasn't sweet. Could I come get her?

At the store, Frosty didn't recognize me when I talked to her. I opened the cage door and she let me pick her up. I held her tightly to my chest and felt her heart beating as fast as mine does during the rare times I get the urge to jog. I put Frosty in a carrier and brought her home. In the bedroom I opened the carrier. It took Frosty a minute to come out. When she recognized her surroundings, she ran to the dresser, but she didn't fit under it—she had grown since she had been gone. She then dodged into a cardboard box that had been a playhouse for the babies. In the morning she came out to play with the Cat Dancer, and when she got close, I snatched her up and held her. She purred.

"Was the hissing an act so you could come back here?" I asked. She wiggled her way out of my arms and was off running. Of course, I couldn't take her back to the pet store again. But did I need another cat? Not really.

Frosty was lonely. She wanted out of the bedroom, but I worried about her fitting in with the house cats. Finally the day came when I opened the door and allowed her to investigate the rest of the house. There was hissing, growling and butt-sniffing but no fights. The little squirt could hold her own. Within days she was one of the gang. She belonged.

Frosty never lost her love of running. Every morning I'd split two cans of food among the house cats in what I call the 'morning feeding frenzy.' As I prepared the plates, Frosty ran.

"You have time for another lap," I'd tell her. She'd take off up the stairs, come back down, loop through the living room and screech to a halt at her self-appointed spot by the stove. She had no problem getting her fair share of the morning treat.

As she got older, I realized Frosty wasn't a flake. She was one of two cats who figured out that if they put a paw on the paper plate with food, it wouldn't slide across the floor as they ate. Frosty also knew her name. I could call her any time from any place, and she would come running.

Frosty wasn't a lap cat; instead, she sat on the chair arm next to me when I watched television or talked on the phone. Sometimes I'd gently try to tip her onto my lap. It was a no-go. She'd jump down and run away, only to return a few seconds later ... and sit on the chair arm. Her favorite place to be when I read was on the back of my chair where she would occasionally nibble my hair.

When Frosty wanted attention, she'd meow incessantly until I stopped whatever I was doing to scratch her head and massage her back.

Looking back, I think Frosty was separated from her

mother too early. She made friends with the foster kittens but was traumatized when they disappeared from her life. What I labeled as flaky was, in fact, a kitten in need of friends, stability and love. But in researching dilute torti, I came across a post with a new-to-me word: tortitude. The word described the unique personality of tortoiseshell cats. *They tend to be strong-willed, a bit hot-tempered, and they can be very possessive of their human. Other words used to describe torties are fiercely independent, feisty and unpredictable.*

That's my Frosty Flake. She's a cat with tortitude.

Frosty holds the plate still with a paw while eating.

Above: Foster cat Lily and her kittens.
Below: The six kittens who arrived at the shelter in a vacuum cleaner box.

Lily and the Love Bugs
or
The Art of Whining

You might be a crazy cat lady if ... you go to an animal shelter to pick up four kittens and end up leaving with 16 kittens.

Opening the door and stepping into my spare bedroom required the skills of a goalie. In my case, however, instead of stopping a speeding puck, the goal was to keep three gray kittens from dodging out of the room.

The kittens were from a high-kill animal shelter north of Grand Rapids. I first saw them Friday, June 12, 2009, when I rode with Jackie, the founder of a local cat rescue, to the county shelter to pick up cats and kittens. The gray babies, about four weeks old, peered at us in silence from their cage. We loaded them into carriers, along with a dozen other cats.

I was carrying the kitten cargo to the car when a shelter worker asked, "You didn't take the kittens in cage 32, did you?"

Jackie told her we were taking all the cats.

"One of the gray kittens bit someone and all four are under quarantine until Monday," the worker said. "You can't take them."

Really? A four-week-old orphan kitten bit someone? Odds are it was hungry and looking to nurse.

I volunteered to make the hour and a half drive to pick them up on Monday morning.

My stomach was in knots during the entire drive back up there. It should have been a relaxing country cruise, but something didn't feel right. I pulled into the shelter's parking lot a few minutes before its nine o'clock opening time and parked next to a pickup truck. When the shelter's closed sign switched to open, a man and two kids got out of the truck. A small boy carried a black kitten.

"Are you dropping her off?" I asked.

Of course, the answer was yes. The longhaired kitten had appeared in their yard over the weekend, and they didn't want a kitten. "Can I have her?" I asked. "I'm from a rescue in Grand Rapids here to pick up cats. We'll find her a good home." The guy didn't care where the kitten went as long as it was gone from his life. I asked the boy if he had named the kitten.

"We call her Whiner," he said.

"Why Whiner?"

"She whines."

The boy was right. As I put the kitten into a carrier in the back of my Subaru, she talked to me—a long, drawn-out whine.

The shelter staff was expecting me. They informed me more kittens had come in on Saturday, and if I wanted them, they were mine. There was another black kitten, this one shorthaired with a white spot on her chest. A longhaired tiger kitten busily played with a cat toy, and, in another cage, three gray tabbies peered at me with big blue eyes. There were no mothers in sight.

The gray kittens I had come for were staring at me, but instead of shiny gray hair and bright eyes, they were grungy looking with dirty matted fur. It looked like they hadn't been bottle-fed over the weekend. A volunteer said they didn't have any kitten food so she gave them canned dog food hoping they would lick the gravy. I loaded all the kittens into carriers and hauled them to my car. I was finalizing paperwork and saying goodbye when a woman walked in with a vacuum cleaner box. I instinctively knew it held kittens. She opened the box and six little faces stared at me.

"Do you want them?" the shelter director asked me. She explained to the woman I was from a cat rescue and the kittens would be in good hands if I took them.

"I don't have any more carriers. Can I have the box?"

The woman said no. She needed her cardboard vacuum cleaner box.

The director offered me a carrier.

As I pulled out of the parking lot, I performed a mental count of the number of kittens packed in my car. The total was 16. My stomach was still in knots, but now I knew why. I pulled off the road and called Jackie.

"Guess how many kittens I have."

"How many?"

Silence greeted my revelation. Finally, Jackie said she was glad I didn't leave any behind. The reason we rescued cats from this particular shelter was because the county had a contract with a USDA Class B animal dealer. In exchange for disposing of the bodies of the shelter's euthanized cats and dogs, the Class B dealer was given his choice of live animals to take from the shelter and sell for research. We hated the idea of cats going to research. Plus, the shelter euthanized unwanted animals by gassing them in a 55-gallon barrel.

Jackie directed me to take the kittens to the Humane Society of Kent County, which had a good track record of finding homes for healthy kittens; the key word being *healthy*. Staff at the humane society looked at the kittens and said four looked healthy: the longhaired tiger and the three gray tabbies. If they took the remaining kittens, they would be humanely euthanized by the end of the day.

The 12 unhealthy-looking kittens, including the original four I volunteered to transport, went home with me.

The gray kittens moved into the bathroom of my spare bedroom. Lily, an adult foster cat, was already camped in the bedroom and sniffed at the bottom of the bathroom door with keen curiosity.

The litter of six went into a cat condo in the garage, and the two black kittens, although unrelated, went together into another cage in the garage.

Jackie came over with antibiotics for the entire troupe. She was concerned about the gray kittens. They should have been bottle fed over the weekend instead of being fed dry, adult cat food and canned dog food. They were hungry.

I went out and bought kitten replacement milk from a nearby veterinarian. Unfortunately, the milk was too late for one of the babies. He wasn't interested in food, not even milk. I begged him to eat, but he faded fast. I buried him that night in my pet cemetery.

The three remaining babies fought over the bottle. One was tinier than the rest and wouldn't eat kitten-chow gravy when it was offered. I'd wrap his grungy little body in a washcloth and hold him in one hand while holding the bottle in the other. He sucked down the milk while staring into my eyes. Within days, he, too, was eating kitten chow.

The babies consumed my time. I worried they weren't eating enough, and I was constantly cheering them to chow down. I sponged their fur to clean it—they were too fragile for baths. When the possibility of death passed, names appeared. The little guy became Smokey Bear. His sister, with a blaze of orange on her nose, was tagged Peaches. The other brother became Love Bug, although all three were love bugs. Together they cuddled on my lap purring in unison.

As they grew, they began sniffing Lily under the bathroom door. Lily, a light gray tabby with white feet and the greenest eyes I've ever seen, was rescued from the northern shelter three months earlier. I had fostered her and her four babies for the local shelter. When the kittens were old enough to be adopted, I dropped mom and her brood at the shelter. I was surprised to get a call four weeks later. Mom was sick and not responding to medication; she was going to be euthanized. I begged that she be returned to me. They relented. I picked her up with two types of medicine to treat upper respiratory infection. She thrived once she was out of the shelter and back home.

Two weeks later Lily watched in disbelief as I let the gray babies wander into her bedroom—she thought she was done with the mothering thing. The kittens looked at her with a gleam in their eyes. I read it as, "Mom, where have you been?" Lily tolerated the intruders for the first two days. Then I caught her sleeping on the bed with the babies ... they blossomed under her care.

Meanwhile, the garage gang outgrew their cages and had the run of the entire structure. I noticed that after I let the black girls run loose with the six siblings, Whiner quit whining. Apparently all she needed was friends.

Soon I was the one whining. My car was parked outside and my pet supply budget had tripled—my free time evaporated with 21 cats and kittens who all complained they didn't get enough back rubs. And the carpeting in the spare bedroom was plagued with litter and cat hair. I paid $110—a surgical steal—to get the gang of 11 neutered and spayed, but that was 20 fewer pizzas for me. And all that was the easy part. I needed to find them homes ... and then I had to say goodbye.

***

Epilogue: The northern shelter no longer gives animals to the USDA Class B dealer and now uses lethal injection for euthanasia. Safe Haven Humane Society accepted the kittens into their adoption program, and I provided a foster home for them until they were adopted. Eight were adopted, but two were returned (including Whiner). I ended up adopting those two plus three others who were shy kitties and couldn't handle being in a cage at adoption events. Since then I have successfully said no to any new cats ... except for one.

Peaches, Smokey Bear and Love Bug.

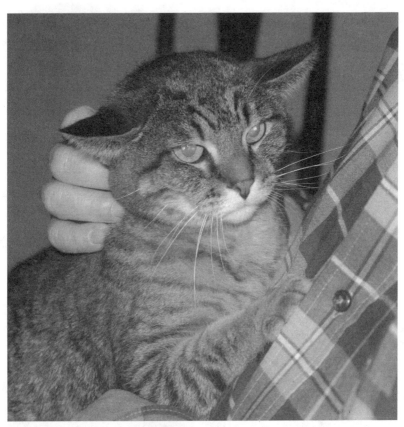

Wild Cat and Leonard.

Dating with Cats

You might be a crazy cat lady if ... you don't tell dates how many cats you have.

"Have you told him how many cats you have?" my sister Rose asked.

Him was a guy named Leonard I had met on match.com. In my profile, I had written that I was an ethical vegetarian—I didn't think it was right to eat animals—and an animal advocate who had more cats than one person should have. My short bio didn't include the specific number of cats.

To my surprise, several of the men who responded selected 'hunting and fishing' as a hobby. One guy from out east planned to retire to Michigan. When I asked why Michigan, he wrote that the mitten state had some of the best fishing around. I then asked if he thought fish felt pain when they got a hook stuck in their mouth. I didn't hear back from him.

My standard reply to the hunters and fishermen became, "Do you think an animal advocate who doesn't eat meat would be a good match with someone who hunts and kills animals?"

Only one guy answered the question. He said, "I've lived on a lake for 15 years and have never fished, and I don't hunt.

I checked 'hunting and fishing' because it was the closest option to my hobby of collecting guns."

I wasn't fond of guns, but after thinking about it, I decided gun collecting wouldn't be a deal breaker. Leonard and I emailed back and forth for a few weeks before taking our relationship to the next level—talking on the phone. Two months after first contact we took it to another level— we met for a date, an outing to Frederik Meijer Gardens & Sculpture Park followed by dinner at Olive Garden.

Rose asked her question after that first date, "Did you tell him how many cats you have?"

"He didn't ask and I didn't tell," I answered.

Leonard's late wife was a dog person, so he's familiar with having critters (as he calls them) in the house. He also had an aunt, long passed, who cared for a barn-full of cats. He reminisces fondly of her and her colony of cats.

Whiner, Wild Cat and Izzy took a fancy to Leonard. Whenever he sat on the couch they squabbled for lap time. During the winter when the fireplace attracted cats like moths to a light bulb, Len could see my feline family. He still didn't ask.

Three years into the relationship, I was going to attend a two-day conference and needed a cat sitter. Len offered. "Just show me what I need to do," he said.

"It involves cleaning litter boxes and feeding and watering cats."

"I think I could handle it."

So he got a lesson in scooping litter and filling food and water bowls.

When I returned he said, "I counted nine."

"That's close," I said. I didn't know if his number included the barn cats or just the house cats. I didn't ask.

Four years into our relationship and Leonard still hasn't asked ... and I still haven't told. But he's an engineer, so I know he can count. Apparently, the number doesn't matter.

Izzy.

Mom Cat aka Izzy

You might be a crazy cat lady if ... you resolve to say no the next time someone tells you her hard-luck story and expects you to take her cat, but then when the time comes to confirm your resolution, you hear yourself saying ... yes.

When Mom Cat—the mother of the six black kittens—was visibly pregnant, a neighbor happened to stop by for a visit. While we talked, the tabby with her bulging belly, strolled by.

"Izzy! What are you doing here?" Nancy said in disbelief.

"Izzy?" I said.

"Isabel. She's my husband's favorite cat. We wondered where she went."

Nancy explained that they had gotten a new dog who Izzy didn't like. Soon afterwards, Izzy, who probably wasn't feeling favored anymore, disappeared. "We keep expecting her to come home, but we'd about given up on her," said Nancy as she scooped up Izzy and cradled her. The hijacked cat didn't object. "Gene will be so glad to see her." And just like that, the expectant mom was gone. I broke the news to Buddy and Rocky, who didn't seem to care, but I did. The barn felt empty without her.

To my delight, the next morning at feeding time, Izzy was back. The neighbors never called or came looking for her; they never even inquired about their grand-kittens.

After the babies were born, Izzy's name evolved into Mom Cat. After the babies were weaned, she was spayed. My intention was for her to be a housecat, but her opinion differed. She insisted on being an outside cat. Whenever a door opened, she was determined to get out and escape the confines of walls, carpeting, furniture and conditioned air. She preferred the sky above her head, grass under her feet, chipmunks to chase and trees to climb.

I finally got the message. "Be a barn cat," I said.

All was well until Wild Cat appeared on the scene and began bullying everyone. Mom Cat weighed her options and decided the dog back at the farm was less of a threat than the young tomcat who had no manners. So Mom Cat returned to her first home. During the next few years, I saw her now and then. Once when she was out for a walk with her people--I knelt and scratched her head and gave her belly rubs when she rolled on her back. It was like seeing a long-lost friend. Another time I spotted her in my yard. I sat on the porch and called her. I lavished her with love, told her how her daughters were doing and how much we missed her. Then she was gone again, which was for the best.

I was coming to my senses. My husband had always limited the number of cats we could have. When the marriage ended, so did his restraint. As captain of my own ship, I could have as many cats as I fancied, but I was slowly realizing it was possible to have too many cats. There's a saying, "Cats are like potato chips, you can't have just one." I can't eat just one potato chip, and I can't have just one cat. But I now know there is a limit to how many cats I can care for, just like there is a limit to how many potato chips I can eat. I worry that my numbers on both accounts are higher than those of most people.

I had enough cats. I was determined to say no the next time the opportunity to add to the family presented itself.

Then came the knock on my door. It was Nancy. "We're moving, and we're not taking Izzy," she said.

"You're moving?"

The recession had hit them hard, and the bank foreclosed on their farm. They didn't know where they were going, but they were taking the dog and not the cat. "I was going to leave her in the barn, but then I thought maybe you would take her," she said.

I heard myself saying, "Of course, I'll take her." How could I not? She was Mom Cat, the beloved mother of my Stretch and Sweetie. Besides, if Nancy left her alone in the barn, Izzy would have made her way to my house when she got hungry.

Nancy just happened to have Izzy in her car—she knew what my answer would be before she even asked. She got Izzy, handed her to me and said goodbye. Just like that, I had another cat.

"Sorry, Izzy," I said, "this time you're going to be a house cat."

The only room in the house that didn't have cats in it was the bathroom, so that's where she went. The necessary amenities were added—litter box, bowls and a bed—but she needed more. By the window I placed a three-step ladder, which had a work platform designed to hold tools or paint. Covered with a folded towel, it would serve as a padded observation deck.

"At least you'll be able to look outside," I told her.

To my surprise, Mom Cat didn't seem to mind. It was early winter and she enjoyed the warmth. Fortunately for her, I used the bathroom frequently so she got plenty of attention. She stayed in the bathroom for a few weeks. She visited with the other house cats under the door, and when the day came that she wanted to venture out, I let her.

Mom Cat fit right in. I expected a happy family reunion when she met Stretch and Sweetie, but I don't think there was any recognition from either mom or daughters, even though Stretch, who was the self-appointed guardian of my bed, allowed Mom Cat to sleep with us, a favor otherwise only granted to Sweetie.

I worried about the first meeting between Wild Cat and Mom Cat, but there was no need to worry. Either they didn't remember their first encounters in the barn or all was forgiven.

As I became reacquainted with Mom Cat, I recognized similarities between her and Stretch. They're both polydactyl. They both use a paw to tap me when I try to ignore their request for attention. They both bite when they get excited. A not-so-good similarity is that they both forget to squat when they pee—they stand in the litter box and the pee streams onto the floor. Is that a genetic trait or a learned behavior?

Sweetie squats, but then she doesn't paw or bite me. I don't know. All I know is, I'm tired of cleaning the floor.

Izzy loves sleeping on flannel sheets, especially on my pillow.

Above: Bad boy Rocky in the catio.
Below: Bad boys Blink and T-bone bird watching.

The Bad Boys Club

You might be a crazy cat lady if ... your computer quits working. You drop it off for repairs and the next day they call and ask, "Do you have a cat?"

The word "pissed" takes on a new meaning when you have an unhappy cat. I'm not sure who started it, but behind my back the boys started a pissing contest—or should I say spraying contest? Spraying is a term used when male cats direct a stream of urine over an object or area to mark their territory.

I'm not sure how long it took me to catch on, but I started to smell it, and when the light was right, I'd see dribbles streaking down the walls. It took me a few days to realize it wasn't only the walls they'd claimed ownership of.

One chilly evening I decided to take a bubble bath in the master bathroom's whirlpool tub. I ran the water, poured in rose scented bath crystals, dimmed the lights, undressed and, at the last minute, turned on the electric heater that sat on the counter. I stepped into the water, settled in, warming and relaxing. Then I noticed the smell. Not the sweet scent of roses. It smelled like ... it took me a minute ... it smelled like ... *burnt cat pee.* It took me another minute to put two and two together. Someone had sprayed the heater and, as the element got hot, it cooked the urine. Did you hear me scream?

A day or two later my desktop computer quit working. It had an extended warranty, so I called and made an appointment to take it to the Apple store. The next day I dropped it off. The following day the phone rang.

"Hello, I'm calling from the Apple store."

"Did you find the problem? Is it fixed?"

"Do you have a cat?"

"Yes."

"Well, we found what we suspect to be cat urine inside the computer. That's why it's not turning on."

"Can you fix it?"

"Well ... no. Cat urine on electronics creates a biohazard, and we're not allowed to work on it."

"What?"

"I'm sorry. We closed it and you'll have to come get it."

"But it's under warranty."

"Cat urine voids the warranty."

I hung up before I screamed.

I wasn't sure who the culprit was, so I bought a trail cam, the kind of camera hunters use to get photographs of wildlife. It was motion activated and worked in low light, but I didn't need the camera to catch Rocky. In a fevered state to mark the living room as his space, he made the mistake of doing the deed while I was not even 15 feet from him. The next day I caught Buddy doing the same thing.

"Why?" I screamed. "I put a roof over your head. Feed you. Clean the litter boxes. This is how you repay me?"

A couple of the bad boys were smart enough not to spray in front of me, which told me they knew what they were doing was a no-no. I set the camera at night and during the day when I was going to be gone for any length of time. Downloading photographs became part of my daily routine. There were dozens of photos of cats walking by, close-ups of cats checking out the camera and sniffing the area. Persistence paid off. Eventually I caught Blink. Then Tiger. Then Geo Cat.

But what to do? Fortunately, I had the barn, but I didn't want outside cats killing my birds, bunnies and chipmunks. The safety of free-roaming cats was also a concern. The wooded ravines behind the house were home to coyotes, fox and other predators. Plus, the Grand River was about a half mile away and bald eagles nested along the banks and, while they love fish, a cat would make a tasty snack.

I Googled 'cat enclosures' and learned a new word: catio, a patio for cats. With the help of my brother, we renovated a portion of the barn for the bad boys. We put up a 2-by-4 frame and stapled mesh fencing over it, enclosing an area the size of a one-stall garage. Bales of hay, leftover from when my horse was alive, were stacked at one end and provided access to the rafters where pieces of plywood created walkways. In the upper level, I placed drawers from an old chest and lined them with towels and cat beds, creating cozy hideouts. I took an old folding door, removed the hinges and used the panels to make a catwalk along one wall.

Leonard helped us enclose a similar sized area outside. I used lumber to make a catwalk around the perimeter and built ramps for the cats to get to the ground. A cat door in a window provided access to the outside catio.

They have a fan for when it gets hot in the summer. Heat lamps hang from the rafters above their beds in preparation for winter. From Amazon, I purchased an electric water bowl.

The Bad Boys Club cost close to $500 to build and furnish.

Rocky was the first to be evicted. Then Buddy. Then Tiger and Blink.

Catching Geo Cat proved to be a challenge. He was smart. He knew something wasn't right when his buddies started disappearing. I'm embarrassed to say I actually caught him and had him in a carrier, but he escaped before I could close the door, and I have the scars to prove it. From then on I couldn't get close to the you're-not-going-to-catch-me bad boy.

While Geo Cat and I were feuding, I happened to interview an animal communicator for an article I was writing. She offered to do a long-distance reading on one of my cats to demonstrate her ability. All she wanted was a name.

"Tell me about Geo Cat," I said. I went into the session a skeptic and came out a believer. She told me that Geo showed her the lifecycle of flowers—little plants growing, maturing and eventually blooming.

"I've never had a cat show me that before. I don't know what it means," she said.

I understood. Geo's favorite place was a chair pushed up to a window that overlooked a small flower garden. The chair was his domain. He sat there. He slept there. He spent hours staring outside.

She told me Geo knew he was in trouble. She guessed it was a litter box issue, a common problem with cats. She explained to him that the house was mine and he needed to live by my rules and one of those rules was using the litter box. If he did that, she assured him I would no longer be upset.

I swear the day she had her "talk" with Geo, he started using the litter box again. To my surprise, he also came and sat on my lap. Something he hadn't done since the carrier fiasco. He looked up at me as if to say, "I get it. I'll use the litter box. Can I stay?"

I told him he could. He forgets now and then. When he does, he avoids me. He knows. So for now, he's still a house cat.

It didn't take long for the other four to get accustomed to being corralled barn cats. Rocky had used a dog door before, so he was able to teach the other three the art of pushing the door open to go outside. Now they can spray all they want, wherever they want.

Daffodils mark Lucy's grave.

Saying Goodbye

You might be a crazy cat lady if ... you have your own pet cemetery with flowers and concrete cat statues marking the graves.

Pet stories which end in death leave me weepy and sad. The stories in this memoir span 30-plus years, so it's inevitable that some of the cats you have read about have passed. If you don't like to read about death and dying, skip this chapter. Feel free to think of all the cats you've met in these pages perpetually sunning themselves, sleeping on my bed and purring.

***

The death of Lucy hit me hard, maybe because it was unexpected. One morning she wasn't waiting for me at the bottom of the stairs. I called and she didn't come. I found her lying on the floor by her food bowl.

"Lucy what are you doing? Are you on a hunt?" I asked.

She didn't move. I spoke her name louder. No response. I bent down and touched her. She was stiff. It took a few seconds to realize she was dead. I backed out of the room and closed the door.

I had a date that morning with a friend to go kayaking. I hurriedly packed my things and left. During the outing I tried to put the incident out of my mind but couldn't. As I drove home my mantra was: "Please let her be alive. Please let her be alive."

She wasn't.

I buried her in the yard and planted daffodils on her grave. Mark left the next day for a two-week job, leaving me alone with my grief. My heart ached, a deep physical pain I carried everywhere. For nine years, Lucy had been the center of my universe.

A friend talked of her dad's death and said she felt his presence when she was quiet. That his spirit was in the wind, the flowers and everything good. Her philosophy comforted me. My grief was for me. Lucy was in heaven, no longer paralyzed, walking on all four feet, chasing mice, chipmunks and birds, but never catching them and not caring that she didn't. Only years later did I realize why Lucy's death was so painful. She filled a void in my life. She was my baby. She needed mothering, and I needed to mother.

Shortly before she died I had seen an ad in the newspaper about a pet loss support group. In my despair I went to a meeting, even though it was in a downtown area unfamiliar to me and held after dark. The therapist who ran the group was absent. I listened to a handful of women who seemed to know each other talk nonstop about everything but the death of pets. The one in charge took my name, address, and telephone number and said the therapist would call. I sat by the phone for a week waiting for that call. I skipped classes and didn't go for walks in anticipation of help. He never called, but I did make the group's mailing list for fundraising.

During that time, I spent countless hours staring mindlessly at the television. It was back when MTV played music videos, and Melissa Etheridge's "I'm the Only One" was popular. The line "I'm the only one who'd walk across fire for you" touched my heart. The song is forever intertwined with Lucy's passing. She died in 1994, and the song still brings tears to my eyes.

Boomer left this world in 2004. He had hyperthyroidism (an overactive thyroid) and was treated with radioactive iodine therapy. The treatment makes cats temporarily radioactive so Boomer had to be hospitalized for a short period afterward. He gained a little weight, but he always remained thin. He eventually became a house cat, and I was able to pamper him during the last couple years of his life. When he quit eating, I kept him comfortable and within a couple days he died in my arms.

Maggie, Buddy, Pearl and Pumpkin have also passed.

For me, euthanasia is a personal decision. Some people question my decision to let my cats die on their own at home, and I think some people are too quick to "end the suffering" of a pet. If they are truly suffering, I understand. But sometimes I question whose suffering they're avoiding. It makes me think of my parents' death. Both died of cancer and had to live until their bodies shut down. Dying on their own was the only end to their suffering.

The most recent cat to pass was Wild Cat. He died June

27, 2016. For months he had been slowly losing weight. Blood work came back normal, but the vet suspected cancer. He said he could do more tests, but if it were cancer there would be no treatment. He said take him home and appreciate the time he had left. So I did.

The day before he passed, Wild Cat was restless. He would walk short distances and then stop to rest. He went outside in the house catio. He loved soaking up the heat of the sun. When I checked on him, he looked guilty, like he had caught something. He did. A snake and it was dead. I screamed. He wanted to bring the bloody corpse into the house, but I wouldn't let him.

That was the last time Wild Cat went outside. The snake was his last kill.

That night he sat on my lap and all was forgiven. When I spoke his name, Wild Cat purred. Whatever caused his decline didn't affect his fur. It was still thick, soft and pleasant to stroke, but underneath every bone could be felt. We watched TV late into the night. I carried him to my bedroom and put him on the bed, thinking he didn't have the strength to jump up. At some point I woke and petted him. He felt cold and, in the fog of sleep, I thought he had passed. I decided to stay in bed and take care of him in the morning. Later I heard a noise—it was Wild Cat jumping off the bed. Apparently he wasn't dead yet. To my surprise the next time I woke, he was back on the bed. In the morning he was missing again. I found him sleeping on the floor in the living room.

He woke and, with the other cats, came to breakfast,

but he didn't eat. He sat by the water bowl but didn't drink. When I left for work, I had a gut feeling he would be gone before I got home, so I said my good-byes, telling him how much he was loved. How much I enjoyed having him in my life, and how much I would miss him. When I came home he was dead, lying on the floor by the door. Had he been waiting for me? I regretted not being there with him for his final breath.

I wrapped Wild Cat in my favorite towel and Leonard helped me bury him next to Buddy. His grave is marked with a cement cat statue. I miss him.

Buddy and Wild Cat's graves marked by
concrete statues.

Dog 281

By Janet Vormittag

Chapter One

Just as I summoned the courage to smash the window, distant headlights and the rumble of an engine interrupted me. I flattened myself belly down among waist-high dead weeds. A security light cast a pale glaze over the renovated red barn and surrounding area, me included. I prayed my form melted into the landscape. A chorus of spring peepers from a nearby swamp camouflaged the pounding of my heart, but I wished my hiding place wasn't ten feet from the kennel's door.

A car pulled into the circular driveway and parked behind a grove of blue spruce. *Did I trip a silent alarm?* The last thing I needed was to explain to my grandmother why her sweet, law-abiding granddaughter was in the county jail. Doors opened, and I heard rock music mingled with voices and laughter. Through the weeds, I could see teenagers. Four of them. They were sitting on the hood and leaning against the fenders, sipping beer and eating pizza. The kennel was situated on an old homestead where trees and overgrown flowerbeds outlined where a house once stood. The seclusion made it a perfect party place for underage drinkers.

I worried the partiers would attract the police and

panicked when a young man stumbled in my direction. He stopped so close I could hear his stream of urine drenching the weeds, and his feel-good sigh of emptying a bladder of spent beer. If there had been a breeze, I would have been sprinkled. I gagged at the pungent smell. It felt like the intruders stayed for hours, but, in fact, it was thirty-four minutes. Thirty-four minutes of my face pressed into musty dry weed stubble, anxious about slithering snakes seeking my body heat and grateful that mosquitoes had not yet hatched. When they drove away, the teenagers left behind a grease-stained pizza box, empty Budweiser cans and me, a nervous, frustrated wreck.

Brushing dirt and dead grass from my sweatshirt and jeans, I got back to work. My first tap on the double-pane window with the ball peen hammer was too timid. The second whack shattered the glass, and it echoed like carillon music as it fell to the concrete floor inside. The nearest neighbor was a half-mile away, so I didn't worry about the noise. Wearing leather gloves, I snapped the leftover shards of glass from the window frame. I stepped on a weathered crate, leaned inside and dropped my backpack and a dog carrier to the concrete floor. Hoisting myself onto the windowsill, I paused to take several deep breaths to calm my nerves. I expected sirens, but all I heard were muffled barks and singing peepers.

Fumbling in my backpack, I retrieved my flashlight and put away the hammer. I switched on the light and its beam pierced the darkness and led me to the metal door that opened into the kennel. When I turned the doorknob and pushed it open, frantic barking assaulted my ears and a hot stuffy stench made me gag. The dogs were frenzied by my midnight visit, and they ricocheted around their wire-mesh cages. The flashlight's narrow shaft of light cast dancing shadows. Not much had changed from that morning. The hodgepodge of dogs were still trapped in filthy pens.

"Take me with you, take me with you," they begged in a doggie language I knew too well.

"Sorry guys," I said. "I'm looking for my dogs Cody and Blue."

At the end of the first row of pens was the closed door that hadn't been part of my earlier tour. Inside, six German shepherds were corralled in a pen. They jumped about, barking with excitement. None wore collars. They looked well-fed and somewhat mannered. In the murky light they all looked alike, but one jumped a little higher and yipped a little louder.

"Sit," I commanded, trying to be heard above the ruckus.

The dog I had raised from a pup obediently sat on his haunches. I opened the gate and Cody sprang forward, not waiting for an invitation. His tail wagged with such force he lost his balance. It was a struggle to keep the other five shepherds from dodging out as well.

"It's so good to see you," I said, ruffling his face between my hands and kissing his cheeks. "Where's Blue?" It was a game we played. Like a typical beagle, Blue would get on the hot scent of who-knows-what and be gone. Cody and I would track him. We searched the rest of the building. We found a room of caged cats that hissed and squirmed when we disrupted their sleep.

Another door led to the interior of the original barn with its wooden cathedral ceiling. It had a stuffy unused smell. I swung my flashlight around the room and saw a Winnebago Motor Home, a shiny red speedboat and two snowmobiles on a trailer. Whatever Gary Jarsma is up to, it must pay well.

Near the door were bags of cat and dog food, cat litter and stacks of dust-laden boxes. In one corner were bales of straw. I wondered why the bedding wasn't in the dog cages. As I turned to leave, I noticed a cardboard box of collars. I picked one up. It was worn leather with two metal tags attached to it; one was a dog license and the other a bone-shaped tag with a name and telephone number stamped in the shiny metal. I stuffed it in my pocket. I searched for Cody and Blue's collars but didn't find them. Most of the collars had tags. I grabbed a handful of them, jammed them inside my backpack and returned to the office. If Blue had already been sold, maybe I could find a record of where he had been shipped. There were three tall file cabinets. Piles of papers were strewn across the desk. In the corner was a copy machine. I flipped it on. As it hummed its warm-up tune, I grabbed what looked to be the most current pile of paperwork and set it in the automatic feed tray. Cody stuck to my side. He had no intention of being left behind.

In one of the cabinets I found a file labeled shipments. The top paper had the previous day's date and listed eight dogs that were sent to Southern Michigan University. I scanned the remaining papers and kept all the ones dated after my dogs went missing. *My dogs—already I thought of them as mine. Maybe Cody was mine, but Blue belonged to my son. Always had. Always would.*

As the papers copied, the constant barking of the caged canines made me wonder what their fate would be. I didn't know any more than what the volunteer at the animal shelter had whispered to me that morning when I checked the shelter for my lost dogs.

"Look at Kappies Kennels," she had said. "He's a licensed animal dealer who sells dogs to research labs." Before I could ask any questions, the shelter director walked into the room and the volunteer scurried away. I introduced myself and asked about my missing dogs. He had me fill out a lost dog report and suggested I come back at least every other day to look for them.

"By law we only have to hold dogs for four days if they come in without a collar or microchip. Did your dogs have collars or were they microchipped?"

"They weren't microchipped. They had collars, but the information on the tags is wrong. I wrote it on the report."

"Collars can come off. We'll keep an eye out for them, but we get busy. You need to walk though the kennels and look for them on your own. You also need to put up some lost dog posters. An ad in the Lost and Found in the newspaper would be a good idea, too."

I thanked him for the suggestions and assured him I would check back at least every other day. He didn't mention dogs being transferred to an animal dealer.

"By the way, my name is Sam Grensward," he said. He read my report as he led me to the kennel area. "You must be Anna's granddaughter."

"I am."

"So how did you lose your dogs?"

"I didn't lose them. Someone took them from Grams' fenced-in yard."

"Why would anyone do that?"

"I don't know. All I know is the gate was closed, but the dogs were gone."

"Maybe you didn't close the gate and they pushed it open."

"I don't think so. The gate latches automatically when it swings closed. We checked. It works fine."

Sam didn't have an answer for the obvious theft of my dogs. He led me through the maze of kennels, and I didn't find Cody or Blue. Since Cindi had already told me they didn't have any beagles or German shepherds, I wasn't surprised. He ushered me to the door.

"Remember to come back."

The comment didn't warrant an answer.

I recalled a green and white sign for Kappies Kennels tucked among towering blue spruce trees in the yard of an abandoned farm on Kirby Road. I drove there as soon as I left the shelter.

A middle-aged man greeted me before I could even get out of my car. He turned out to be the owner, Gary

Jarsma, a balding, haggard looking bone-thin man with John Lennon wire-rim glasses.

"I'm Alison Cavera, and I'm looking for a couple lost dogs. A German shepherd and a beagle." His stare made me feel guilty. Guilty for looking for my own dogs. "They disappeared two days ago from my grandmother's house near Pearline."

"I don't think I have any shepherds or beagles, but you can look after you fill out a visitor's form. Wait here. I'll be right back." He turned and walked through an open garage door into a pole barn where I could see him talking with a young man. A couple minutes later he returned and handed me a clipboard and pen.

"If you don't mind, just fill this out."

The form asked for my name, address, telephone number and what type of animals I was looking for. He waited as I filled in the answers. When I finished, I handed it to him.

"They have collars, but the information on the tags is old. I just moved here." He wrote a note on the form, and then asked for my driver's license.

"Why?"

"Security. If you want in, I see your license."

I retrieved it from my purse. Jarsma compared the license data to what I had written. He scribbled my Chicago address next to Gram's address. He handed the license back to me.

"Follow me," he said, leading me into the pole barn and through a one-desk office. I scurried to keep up with him. As he swung open a heavy metal door, I was assaulted by a musty stench and the uproar of excited animals who sounded like they had been caged too long. He pointed to an aisle.

"Go ahead, take a look."

In the first pen a brownish-black terrier leaped and bounced off the front of its wire-mesh run. Next to it was a shepherd mix. Then a black lab-like dog with white paws who danced in circles. There were puddles of urine and piles of feces on the cement floor. In each pen there was a grimy food bowl and a coffee can partially filled with water.

I held my breath and hurried to the end of the aisle as Jarsma followed close behind. In the last pen five reddish-brown puppies tumbled over each other in play. Jarsma guided me around the corner and pointed to another walkway with pens on both sides. More dogs, some two and three to a pen. I didn't look too closely. All I wanted was to find Cody and Blue. I didn't.

"I didn't think we had your dogs, but if any shepherds or beagles come in I'll give you a call," Jarsma said as he walked me to my car.

"What do you do with these dogs?"

"They're used in medical schools, veterinarian schools, research labs. They'd be put to sleep at the shelter. Might as well use them to find a cure for cancer or something."

"But aren't they pets?"

"Not any more."

I got into my car and headed home. On the way I listened

to the messages on my cell. One was from Cindi Owens, the volunteer at the shelter. She wanted me to call her at home. I pulled to the side of the road and called her.

"Hi Cindi? It's Alison. Did you find my dogs?"

"No, I just wanted to tell you that if you go to Kappies, don't tell him what kind of dogs you're looking for. I've heard that if he has your dog, he'll hide it in a back room so you can't find it."

"I just came from there."

"Did you find them?"

"No, but why would he lie?"

"He gets about $600 per dog. It's big money out of his pocket if he gives you your dog back."

"I don't believe it."

"I'm just telling you what I heard."

"Where does he sell them?"

"Wherever he can. There's a couple research labs near Kalamazoo, and several universities buy from him."

"For what?"

"Teaching. Research. Testing."

"Isn't that illegal?"

"Jarsma is licensed by the United States Department of Agriculture and has a Class B license. It means he can get animals from random sources and sell them wherever he wants."

"Random sources?"

"Shelters, pets people no longer want, other dealers. The county has a contract with him. Jarsma disposes of the bodies of euthanized animals in exchange for his pick of live dogs and cats. He's in here two or three times a week, checking out what we have."

"Do you think he steals dogs?"

"Nobody has proved it, but a lot of people suspect it. I've heard he doesn't ask questions when people bring him dogs. He pays $50 apiece. Some guys steal dogs for spending money. And in this bad economy, people who can't afford to keep pets are looking for new homes for them. Anybody who is a halfway decent liar can get as many free-to-good-home dogs as he wants."

She added that two other people had been in the shelter in the last week looking for beagles. "I bet he has an order for beagles."

As I hung up, I recalled my visit to the kennel. I could see Jarsma talking to a teenage boy and then coming out and having me fill out the paperwork. I had already told him what kind of dogs I was looking for. Could that young kid have been hiding Cody and Blue as I filled out the search forms? I recalled seeing dirty empty kennels, which was odd when some kennels held several dogs. Damn him.

As I finished copying the files, I felt a twinge of guilt at rescuing Cody and leaving the other animals behind. Then it came to me, like an early-morning insight you get when showering, I couldn't take the other dogs with me, but I didn't have to leave them in this stink hole. I already planned on rescuing the adorable pups.

Back at their pen, two of them cuddled on a filthy orange blanket while the other three sniffed my ankles when I stepped inside their kennel.

"Come here you cute little babies. Where's your mama?" I said, as one by one I plopped them into the carrier. With the puppies safe and my backpack stuffed with papers, I looked around and took a moment to think of any clues to my identity I was leaving behind. I wore gloves so I didn't leave fingerprints. I did a mental count of the tools, and they were all accounted for. Maybe the pizza box and beer cans would help cover my activities. At the least, they would be misleading.

I propped open a side door. With Cody tagging along, I squeezed open the clips holding the cage doors shut. It took about 20 minutes to open all the kennels. With the fresh night air beckoning, the dogs ignored me and raced to freedom.

In the cat room, I opened a window before swinging the cage doors open. The cats hesitated. I caught a brown tabby and perched him on the windowsill. It didn't take him long to leap to freedom. Next I sat a calico in the window. The other cats watched as she disappeared outside. I helped two other cats onto the windowsill and left before they jumped. I could only hope the rest of the cats would escape after I left. I felt confident the fresh air and night sounds would entice them outside.

As I hiked to my car, parked on a two-track dirt road that ran alongside a nearby cornfield, I could see dogs sniffing around the yard and a couple cats dodging into a neighboring hay field. I had to hustle and get cruising before a vehicle came down Kirby Road and spotted the menagerie of animals.

One dog clung to Cody's side, and when I opened the car door he hopped in the back seat while Cody assumed his navigation post in the passenger seat. The newcomer's big brown eyes pleaded with me not to evict him from the car. I didn't have the heart to order him out. I put the carrier with its puppy cargo in the back seat, along with my backpack. As I drove away, dogs and cats were everywhere. *Run.* I thought. *Run as far and fast as you can.*

If you'd like to read more, *Dog 281*, and its sequel, *More Than a Number*, can be purchased online at www. janetvormittag.com or at www.amazon.com.

Shipping is free (via media mail) if purchased with the order form below and paid with check or money order.

Dog 281 .... $13.95 x _____ = _____

More Than a Number .... $13.95 x _____ = _____

You might be a Crazy Cat Lady if... $13.95 x _____ = _____

TOTAL .... _____ _____

Mail check (made out to Janet Vormittag) or money order to:

Cats and Dogs
P.O. Box 996
Jenison, MI 49429-0996

Dog 281 .... $13.95 x _____ = _____

More Than a Number .... $13.95 x _____ = _____

You might be a Crazy Cat Lady if... $13.95 x _____ = _____

TOTAL .... _____ _____

Mail check (made out to Janet Vormittag) or money order to:

Cats and Dogs
P.O. Box 996
Jenison, MI 49429-0996

With *You Might be a Crazy Cat Lady if ...*, Janet Vormittag is coming out of the closet as a Crazy Cat Lady. Janet has a bachelor's degree in journalism from Grand Valley State University and was a correspondent for the *Grand Rapids Press* for ten years. She is the publisher and editor of *Cats and Dogs, a Magazine Devoted to Companion Animals*, which she founded in 2006. Janet is also the author of two novels, *Dog 281* and its sequel, *More Than a Number*. In her free time, Janet enjoys geocaching, kayaking, hiking, gardening and being a member of Toastmasters. Janet lives in West Michigan with ... her cats.

www.janetvormittag.com